D1316419

Disneyland's Hidden Mickeys

Third Edition

DISNEYLAND'S HIDDEN MICKEYS

A Field Guide to

Disneyland Resort®'s

Best Kept Secrets

Third Edition

Steven M. Barrett

DISNEYLAND'S HIDDEN MICKEYS

A Field Guide to Disneyland® Resort's
Best Kept Secrets
3rd edition

Published by
The Intrepid Traveler
P.O. Box 531
Branford, CT 06405
http://www.intrepidtraveler.com

Copyright ©2011 by Steven M. Barrett
Third Edition
Printed in the U.S.A.
Cover design by Foster & Foster
Interior Design by Starving Artist Design Studio
Maps designed by Evora Taylor
Library of Congress Card Number: 2011930043
ISBN-13: 978-1-887140-93-5

All rights reserved. No part of this book may be reproduced or transmitted in any form or by any means, electronic or mechanical, including photocopying, recording, or by any information storage and retrieval system, without the express written permission of the publisher, except for the inclusion of brief quotations in a review.

10 9 8 7 6 5 4 3 2 1

Trademarks, Etc.

This book makes reference to various Disney copyrighted characters, trademarks, marks and registered marks owned by The Walt Disney Company and Disney Enterprises, Inc.

All references to these properties, and to The Twilight Zone®, a registered trademark of CBS, Inc. are made solely for editorial purposes. Neither the author nor the publisher makes any commercial claim to their use, and neither is affiliated with either The Walt Disney Company or CBS, Inc. in any way.

Photo by Vickie Barrett

About the Author

Author Steven M. Barrett, a Texas native, Air Force veteran, and former University of Oklahoma professor, paid his first visit to Disneyland as a child. He has hunted Hidden Mickeys at Disneyland for years and wrote his first *Disneyland's Hidden Mickeys* book in 2007. Because new Hidden Mickeys appear over time and others are lost, he updates the book every few years. In this book, you'll find a Hidden Mickey Scavenger Hunt for each of the theme parks, along with a third hunt that includes Downtown Disney, the resort hotels, and other areas on Disneyland property. To organize the Scavenger Hunts for efficient touring, Steve consulted various guidebooks and conducted his own research.

Dedication

I dedicate this book to my wife Vickie and our son Steven, who support and help me with my Hidden Mickey passion, and to the many wonderful Hidden Mickey fans I've met through my website and in the Disney parks.

True to their name, Hidden Mickeys are elusive. New ones appear from time to time and some old ones disappear (see page 23, paragraph 2). When that happens—and it will—Steve will let you know on his web site:

www.HiddenMickeysGuide.com

So if you can't find a Mickey—or if you're looking for just a few more—be sure to check it out.

Table of Contents

Acknowledgements 11

Read This First! 15

1. Hidden Mickey Mania 17

2. Disneyland Park Scavenger Hunt 25
   Hints Begin 45

3. Disney California Adventure Scavenger Hunt 67
   Hints Begin 79

4. Downtown Disney District and Resort Hotel Scavenger Hunt 91
   Hints Begin 103

5. Other Mickey Appearances 113

6. My Favorite Hidden Mickeys 115
   My Top Ten 115
   Ten Honorable Mentions 117

Don't Stop Now! 119

Index to Mickey's Hiding Places 121

Maps

Disneyland Park 26
Disney California Adventure Park 68
Disneyland Resort 92

Acknowledgements

No Hidden Mickey hunter works alone. While I've spotted most of the Hidden Mickeys in this book on my own—and personally verified every single one of them—finding Hidden Mickeys is an ongoing group effort. I am indebted to the following dedicated Hidden Mickey lovers for alerting me to a number of Hidden Mickeys I might otherwise have missed. Thanks to each and every one of you for putting me on the track of one or more of these Disneyland treasures and, in some cases, also helping me verify them.

Those named in bold letters have spotted 10 or more, which includes current as well as lost Hidden Mickeys. You can find each person's contribution(s) by visiting my website, www.HiddenMickeysGuide.com. **Extra special thanks to Rosemary and Neil (FindingMickey.com)** for spotting and helping me verify over 140 Hidden Mickeys at Disneyland **and to Sharon Dale** for finding over 50.

Karlos Aguilera, Jonathan Agurcia, Kala'i Ahlo-Souza, The Alberti's, David Almanza, Antonio Altamirano, Bob Anderson, Katrina Andrews, Vahe Arevshatian, Cheryl Armstrong, John Axtell, Kristi B., Brian Babcock, Duane Baker, Hans Balders, Matt and Shelly and Keira Barbieri, Katharine and Ammon Barney, Melisa Beardslee, John Benavidez II, Daniel and Elise Berdin, **Brian Bergstrom**, Jenny Bigpond, **Murray Bishop**, Tina Blaylock, Tim Bonanno, Jacob Steven Bonillas, Lynn Boyd, Lori Brackett, Erik Bratlien, Vicky Braun, Carol Brown, Kaden Brown, Keller Brown, Nicolas Brown, Peter Brown, Thierry and Gabriella and Matthieu Bruxelle, Michael Buell, Marjorie Burns, Felix Bustos, Amy C., Peter C., Chris Caflisch, Bev Cain, Stacy Campbell, Craig Canady, Marisa Cardenas, Nicholas Noah Carreno, Peter Cefalu, Gail Chambers, Leonard Chan, Austin Chanu, Danielle Chard, Chelsi Chipps, Emmy Christopherson, Diana Cimadamore, John Clover, Jeffrey Colwell, Catherine Conroy, Megan Cook, Michelle Cornelius, Marissa Covarrubias, **Josh and Cassi Cox**, **Sharon Dale**, Carlos de Alba, Jessica de la Vara, Jeremiah Dempsey, Jacob DePriest, Tim Devine, Matt Dickerson, Casey Dietz, Thea Dodge, Phillip Donnelly,

Tom Donnelly, Maria Dufault, Lindsey E., Michael Early, Chad Elliot, Scott Evans, Joel Feria, Troy and Cheyanne Field, Rob Fitzpatrick, Nicholas Fleming, Joe Flowers, Melissa Forte, Keitaro Francisco, Ben G., Michele Galvez, Jon Gambill, Valerie Garren, **Sharon Gee**, Sam Gennawey, Staci Gleed, Alec Goldberg, Jimmy Golden, Micheline Golden, Reyna Gonzalez, Jordan Goodman, Alex Goslar, Michael Greening, Josh Grothem, Kimberly Gryte, Carl H., Dave H., Elaine H., Josh and Alyssa and Melody Hadeen, Michael Hadlock, Holly Haider, John Hall, Sarah Hall, The Hallak Family, Jon Handler, Chris Hansen, Cynthia Hess, Kate Heylman, Carl Hoffman, Paul Hoffman, **Milton Holecek**, Michael Hollingsworth, Chas Howell, Cory Hughes, Robert Huntington, Molly Jane, Loren Javier, **Mike Johansen**, James Johnson, Amy Jones, Michelle June, Gordon K., Matt K., Tom K., Summer Kane, Jennifer Kanihan, **Mehlanie Kayra**, Della Kingsland, Xela Knarf, Andrew Knight, Matthew and Missy Knoll, Dalia Kuarez, Meghan Kueny-Thornburg, Chase L., Rhonda Lampitt, Ledawn Larsen, Phillip Lemon, Andrew Lepire, Tony Lepore, Annie Lin, Ronald Lindberg, Alysia Lippetti, Myrna Litt, Ryan Lizama, Allison Lloyd, Joe Loecsey, Amber Lopez, Katherine Lugo, Sal Lugo, Christina M., Henry Macall, Hank Mahler, Maria Maki, C. Mallonee, Jorge Mario, John Martinez, Juan M. Martinez III, Paul Martinez, Dave Marx, **Michael Mason**, Kim McClaughry, Ciara McGovern, James Mcguine, Cindy McKeown, Sylvia McNeil, The Miles Family, Randi Miller, Robert Miller, Christopher Morales, Jose Moran, Carlos Moreno, Danny Mui, The Muklewicz Family, Lindsey Naizer, Bobby Naus, Andy Neitzert, A. Nelson, Aly Nelson, Aryn Nelson, Marina Nelson, Dave and Kim Ness, Ty Nielson, Joseph Nolan, Jen O'Bryan, Elaine Ojeda, Michael and Wendy Olayvar, Jennifer Oliphant, *Orlando Attractions* magazine, Greg Ostravich, Andrew P., Joey P., Monica Garcia Montero P., Sam P., Priscilla Padilla, Shawna Park, Steve Parmley, Justin Parnell, Cherna Patterson, Cheyenne Pemberton, Rob and Buffy and Anna and Julia Penttila, Jennifer Peterson, Christopher Phelan, Eric Polk, Roger Pollard, Diana Poncini, Heather Pone, Robert Powers, Melanie Price,

Alyssa Proudfoot, Marv R., Louise Rafferty, BJ Ralphs, Caleb Richards, Linda Richards, Marv Richards, Joy E. Robertson-Finley, Jeff Robinson, Jose Rodriguez, Katie Rogers, Geoff Rogos, Shaun Rosen, Jean Rowley, Jessica Ruggles, Caleb Ruiz, Richard Ruiz, **Russ Rylee**, John Salinas, Jennifer Salvatierra, Bianca and Nathan and Isaac Santaro, Brandie Sargent, Andy Schelb, Zod Schultz, P. Schwarz, Chris Scott, Kira Scott, Tim Scott, Lauren Seibert, Khrys Sganga, Michael Shearin, Mark Sheppard, The Sherrick Family, Zach Simes, Amy Simpson, Breana Nicole Smith, Rebecca Smith, Jose Solano, Braden Stanley, Brad Steinbrenner, Lloyd Stevens, Darrell St. Pierre, Taylor Stratton, Tyler Struck, Erin T., Mitch T., Donna Taing, Pat Tee, Craig R. Thompson, Sheryl Thompson, Joseph Thorne, Sandy Thornton, Andrew Thorp, The Tierney Family, Tim Titus, Micaela Tracy, Mark Treiger, Eric Upah, Christian Urcia, **Luis Valdez**, Ryan Valle, Kim Vander Dussen, Jeff Van Ry, Aldo Velez, Evelyn Vides, Juliet Violette, Fred Vosecky, Heather W., Ron W., Brock Waidmann, Mel Waidmann III, Melvin Waidmann II, Rhonda Waidmann, William Waidmann, Barrie and Jack Waldman-Marker, Yvonne Washburn, Christopher Williams, Deb Wills, Ken Wilson, Emily Woods, Gracie Wright, Laura Wright, Jeanine Yamanaka, Lynn Yaw, and Monique Zimmer.

AJ, Alan, Alex, Alexz, Amber, Angel, Audrey, Austin, BP, Brittany, Burley, Cathy, Celandra, Cherna, Chris, Christopher, C.J., C.K., Cori, Danny, Derrick, Destiny, Elizabeth, Emily, Eric, **Eric and Colleen and Julie**, Evan, Hans, Hayley, Heather, **Helen and Danny**, Imp, Informer, JC, Jessica, Jonathan, Josh, Julie, Justin, Kelsey, Kendra, Kevin, Kim, Krister, KS and CK, Laura, Laura and Lily, Lea Ann, Lloyd, Lori, **Mari**, Mark, Matt, Matthew, Meg, Megan, Melissa, Michaela, Mike, M.L., Morgan, Nathan, Nicky, Nix, Nusy, Olivia, Peter, Pinky, Queenkoalaandme, Rachel, RaeLynn, Rhonda, **Rosemary and Neil (FindingMickey.com)**, Ryan, Sam, Sandy, Sarah, Sawyer, Scott, Seeing, Serena, Shannon, Shaun, Stephanie, Sylvia, **Tamera**, Taylor, Teressa, Toneto and Laura and Steph, Ty, **Where's Mickey (myspace.com/wheresmickey)**, Zod, and Zoe.

Read This First!

My guess is that you have visited Disneyland before, perhaps many times. But if I've guessed wrong, and this is your first visit, then this note is for you.

Searching for Hidden Mickeys is lots of fun. But it's not a substitute for letting the magic of Disney sweep over you as you experience the Disneyland parks for the first time. For one thing, the scavenger hunts I present in this book do not include all the attractions in the Disneyland theme parks. That's because some of them don't have Hidden Mickeys! For another, the first-time visitor should get ready for fun by also consulting a general Disneyland Resort guidebook for descriptions of Disneyland attractions, shows, dining, and other tourist information.

That doesn't mean you can't search for Hidden Mickeys, too. Just follow the suggestions in Chapter One of this book for "Finding Hidden Mickeys Without Scavenger Hunting."

CHAPTER 1

Hidden Mickey Mania

Have you ever marveled at a "Hidden Mickey"? People in the know often shout with glee when they recognize one. Some folks are so involved with discovering them that Hidden Mickeys can be visualized where none actually exist. These outbreaks of Hidden Mickey mania are confusing to the unenlightened. So let's get enlightened!

Here's the definition of an official Hidden Mickey: a partial or complete image of Mickey Mouse that has been hidden by Disney's Imagineers and artists in the designs of Disney attractions, hotels, restaurants, and other areas. These images are designed to blend into their surroundings. Sharp-eyed visitors have the fun of finding them.

The practice probably started as an inside joke among the Imagineers (the designers and builders of Disney attractions). According to Disney guru Jim Hill (www.JimHillMedia.com), Hidden Mickeys originated in the late 1970s or early 1980s, when Disney was building Epcot and management wanted to restrict Disney characters like Mickey and Minnie to Walt Disney World's Magic Kingdom. The Imagineers designing Epcot couldn't resist slipping Mickeys into the new park, and thus "Hidden Mickeys" were born. Guests and "Cast Members" (Disney employees) started spotting them and the concept took on a life of its own. Today, Hidden Mickeys are anticipated in any new Disney construction anywhere, and Hidden Mickey fans can't wait to find them.

Hidden Mickeys come in all sizes and many forms. The most common is an outline of Mickey's head formed by three intersecting circles, one for Mickey's round head and two for his round ears. Among Hidden Mickey fans, this image is known as the "classic" Hidden Mickey, a term I will adopt in this book. Other Hidden Mickeys include a side or oblique (usually three-quarter) profile of Mickey's face and head, a side profile of his entire body, a full-length silhouette of his body seen from the front, a detailed picture of his face or body, or a three-dimensional Mickey Mouse. Sometimes just his gloves, handprints, shoes, or ears appear. Even his name or initials in unusual places may qualify as a Hidden Mickey.

And it's not just Mickeys that are hidden. The term "Hidden Mickey" also applies to hidden images of other popular characters. There are Hidden Minnies, Hidden Donald Ducks, Hidden Goofys, and other Hidden Characters in the Disneyland Resort, and I include many of them in this book.

The sport of finding Hidden Mickeys is catching on and adds even more interest to an already fun-filled Disneyland vacation. This book is your "field guide" to nearly 400 Hidden Mickeys in the Disneyland Resort. To add to the fun, instead of just describing them, I've organized them into three scavenger hunts, one for each of the theme parks and one for all the rest of the Disneyland Resort: Downtown Disney District, the resort hotels, and beyond. The hunts are designed for maximum efficiency so that you can spend your time looking for Mickey rather than cooling your heels in lines. Follow the Clues and you will find the best Hidden Mickeys Disneyland has to offer. If you have trouble spotting a particular Hidden Mickey (some are extraordinarily well camouflaged!) you can turn to the Hints at the end of each scavenger hunt for a fuller description.

Scavenger Hunting for Hidden Mickeys

To have the most fun and find the most Mickeys, follow these tips:

★ **Arrive early** for the theme park hunts, say 30 minutes before the official opening time. Pick up a Guidemap and Times Guide and plot your course. Then look for Hidden Mickeys in the waiting area while you wait for the rope to drop. You'll find the clues for those areas by checking the *Index to Mickey's Hiding Places* in the back of this book. Look under "Entrance areas." You'll notice that headliner attractions are the first stops in the scavenger hunts. If you arrive later in the day, you may want to pick up a FASTPASS for the first major attraction and then skip down a few clues to stay ahead of the crowd.

★ "Clues" and "Hints"

Clues under each attraction will guide you to the Hidden Mickey(s). If you have trouble spotting them, you can turn to the Hints at the end of the hunt for a fuller description. The Clues and Hints are numbered consecutively, that is, Hint 1 goes with Clue 1; so it's easy to find the right Hint if you need it. In some cases, *Soarin' Over California* in Disney California Adventure for example, you may have to ride the attraction more than once to find all the Hidden Mickeys.

★ Scoring

All Hidden Mickeys are fun to find, but all Hidden Mickeys aren't the same. Some are easier to find than others. I assign point values to Hidden Mickeys, identifying them as easy to spot (a value of 1 point) to difficult to find the first time (5 points). I also consider the complexity and uniqueness of the image: the more complex or unique the Hidden Mickey, the higher the point value. For example, some of the easy-to-spot Hidden Mickeys in Mickey's Toontown in Disneyland are one- or two-point Mickeys. The brilliantly camouflaged Mickey hiding in the tree on one of the ceramic panels decorating a column outside Disney's Grand Californian Hotel & Spa is a five-pointer.

★ Playing the game

You can hunt solo or with others; competitively or just for fun. There's room to tally your score in the guide. Families with young children may want to focus on one- and two-point Mickeys that the little ones will have no trouble spotting. (Of course, little ones tend to be sharp-eyed, so they may spot familiar shapes before you do in some of the more complex patterns.) Or you may want to split your party into teams and see who can rack up the most points (in which case, you'll probably want to have a copy of this guide for each team).

Of course, you don't have to play the game at all. You can simply look for Hidden Mickeys in attractions as you come to them (see "Finding Hidden Mickeys Without Scavenger Hunting" below).

★ Following the clues

The hunts often call for crisscrossing the parks. This may seem illogical at first, but trust me, it will keep you ahead of the crowd. Besides, it adds to the fun of the hunt and, if you're playing competitively, keeps everyone on their toes.

★ Waiting in line

Don't waste time in lines. If the wait is longer than 15 minutes, get a FASTPASS (if available and you're eligible), move on to the next attraction, and come back at your FASTPASS time. Exception: In some attractions, the Hidden Mickey(s) can only be seen from the Standby (regular) queue line, and not from the FASTPASS line. (I've not suggested FASTPASS in the Clues section when that is the case.) The lines at these attractions should not be too long if you start your scavenger hunt when the park opens and follow the hunt clues as given. If you do encounter long lines, come back later during a parade or in the hour before the park closes. Alternatively, if you need to board an attraction with a long wait without a FASTPASS, use the Single Rider queue if available (check your Guidemap for a big "S" symbol next to the attraction).

★ Playing fair

Be considerate of other guests. Some Hidden Mickeys are in restaurants and shops. Ask a Cast Member's permission before searching inside sit-down restaurants, and avoid the busy mealtime hours unless you are one of the diners. Tell the Cast Members and other guests who see you looking around what you're up to, so they can share in the fun.

Finding Hidden Mickeys Without Scavenger Hunting

If scavenger hunts don't appeal to you, you don't have to use them. You can find Hidden Mickeys in the specific rides and other attractions you visit by using the *Index to Mickey's Hiding Places* in the back of this book. For easy lookup, attractions are also listed under their appropriate "lands" (for example, Frontierland in Disneyland and Hollywood Pictures Backlot in Disney California Adventure). To find Hidden Mickeys in the attraction, restaurant, hotel, or shop you are visiting, turn to the *Index*, locate the appropriate page, and then follow the Clue(s) to find the Hidden Mickey(s).

Caution: You won't find every attraction, restaurant, hotel, or shop in the Index. Only those with confirmed Hidden Mickeys are included in this guide.

Hidden Mickeys: Real or Wishful Thinking?

The classic (three-circle) Mickeys are the most controversial, for good reason. Much debate surrounds the gathering of circular forms throughout Disneyland. The three cannonball craters in the wall of the fort in *Pirates of the Caribbean* (Clue 37 in the Disneyland Park Scavenger Hunt) is obviously the work of a clever artist. However, three-circle configurations occur spontaneously in art and nature, as in collections of grapes, tomatoes, pumpkins, bubbles, oranges, cannonballs, and the like. Unlike the cannonball crater Hidden Mickey in *Pirates of the Caribbean*, it may be difficult to attribute a random "classic Mickey" configuration of circles to a deliberate Imagineer design.

So which groupings of three circles qualify as Hidden Mickeys as opposed to wishful thinking? Unfortunately, no master list of actual or "Imagineer-approved" Hidden Mickeys exists. Purists demand that a true classic Hidden Mickey should have proper proportions and positioning. The round head must be larger than the ear circles (so that three equal circles in the proper alignment would not qualify as a Hidden Mickey). The head and ears must be touching and in perfect position for Mickey's head and ears.

On the other hand, Disney's recent mantra is: "If the guest thinks it's a Hidden Mickey,

then by golly it is one!" Of course, I appreciate Disney's respect for their guests' opinions. However, when the subject is Hidden Mickeys, let's apply some guidelines. My own criteria are looser than the purist's but stricter than the "anything goes" Disney approach. I prefer to use a few sensible guidelines.

To be classified as a genuine classic Hidden Mickey, the three circles should satisfy the following criteria:

1. Purposeful (sometimes you can sense that the circles were placed on purpose).

2. Proportionate sizes (head larger than the ears and somewhat proportionate to the ears).

3. Round or at least "roundish."

4. The ears don't touch each other, and the ears are above the head (not beside it).

5. The head and ears touch or they're close to touching.

6. The grouping of circles is exceptional or unique in appearance.

7. The circles are hidden or somewhat hidden and not obviously décor (decorative).

Having spelled out some ground rules, allow me now to bend them in one instance. Some Hidden Mickeys are sentimental favorites with Disney fans, even though they may actually represent "wishful thinking." (My neighbor, Lew Brooks, calls them "two-beer" Mickeys.) Who am I to defy tradition? For example, the three circles on the back of the turtle in *Snow White's Scary Adventures* (Clue 92 in the Disneyland Scavenger Hunt) form a not-quite-proportionate "classic" Mickey. However, if you ask Cast Members near this attraction about a Hidden Mickey, they'll whisper to you these cryptic words: "Watch for the turtle!"

Hidden Mickeys vs. Decorative Mickeys

Some Mickeys are truly hidden, not visible to the tourist. They may be located behind the scenes, available only to Cast Members. You won't find them in this field guide, as I only include Hidden Mickeys that are accessible to the guest. Other Mickeys are decorative; they were placed in plain sight to enhance the décor. For example, in a restaurant, I consider a pat of butter shaped like Mickey Mouse to be a decorative (aka décor) Mickey. Disneyland is loaded with decorative Mickeys. You'll find images of Mickey Mouse on items ranging from manhole covers, to laundry room soap dispensers, to toilet paper wrappers and shower curtains in the hotels. I do not include these ubiquitous and sometimes changing images in this book unless they are unique or hard to spot.

Hidden Mickeys can change or be accidentally removed over time, by the processes of nature or by the continual cleaning and refurbishing that goes on at Disneyland. For example, a classic Mickey on an outside duct at *MuppetVision 3-D* was painted over and is no longer with us. Cast Members themselves sometimes create or remove Hidden Mickeys.

My Selection Process

I trust you've concluded by now that Hidden Mickey Science is an evolving specialty. Which raises the question, how did I choose the nearly 400 Hidden Mickeys in the scavenger hunts in this guide? I compiled my list of Hidden Mickeys from all the resources to which I had access: my own sightings, sightings sent to me by others (see "Acknowledgements"), websites, books, and Cast Members. (Cast Members in each specific area usually—but not always!—know where some Hidden Mickeys are located.) Then I embarked on my verification hunts, asking for help along the way from generous Disney Cast Members. I have included only those Hidden Mickeys I could personally verify.

Furthermore, some Hidden Mickeys are visible only intermittently or only from certain vantage points in ride vehicles. I don't generally include these Mickeys, unless I feel that adequate descriptions will allow anyone to find them. So the scavenger hunts include only those images I believe to be recognizable as Hidden Mickeys and visible to the general touring guest. It is quite likely, though, that one or more of the Hidden Mickeys described in this book will disappear over time.

I'll try to let you know when I discover that a Hidden Mickey has disappeared for good by posting the information on my website:

www.HiddenMickeysGuide.com

If you find one missing before I do, I hope you'll let me know by emailing me care of my website.

I have enjoyed finding each and every Hidden Mickey in this book. I'm certain I'll find more as time goes by, and I hope you can spot new Hidden Mickeys during your visit.

So put on some comfortable walking shoes and experience the Disneyland Resort like you never have before!

Happy Hunting!

— *Steve Barrett*

CHAPTER 2

Disneyland Park Scavenger Hunt

★ Arrive at the entrance turnstiles (with your admission ticket) 30 to 40 minutes before the official opening time.

★ Search for one or more of the following Hidden Mickeys in the ***security bag check area*** if you have plenty of time before the park opens; otherwise, look for them when you leave the park.

Clue 1: Study the signs above you for a classic Mickey on a key chain.
4 points

Clue 2: Now search the signs for a classic Mickey on a ride vehicle.
4 points

Clue 3: Find Mickey ears on Timon and Pumbaa in two different signs.
4 points for both

Clue 4: Locate two more signs with Mickey ears.
4 points for both

Clue 5: As soon as you pass through the ***entrance turnstiles***, look around for a classic Mickey.
3 points

★ Go to *Space Mountain* in Tomorrowland and get a FASTPASS for later.

★ Then walk toward the ***Matterhorn Bobsleds*** in Fantasyland.

Clue 6: Search the mountain for Mickey.
4 points

★ Line up for the *Bobsleds* ride in the right-hand queue.

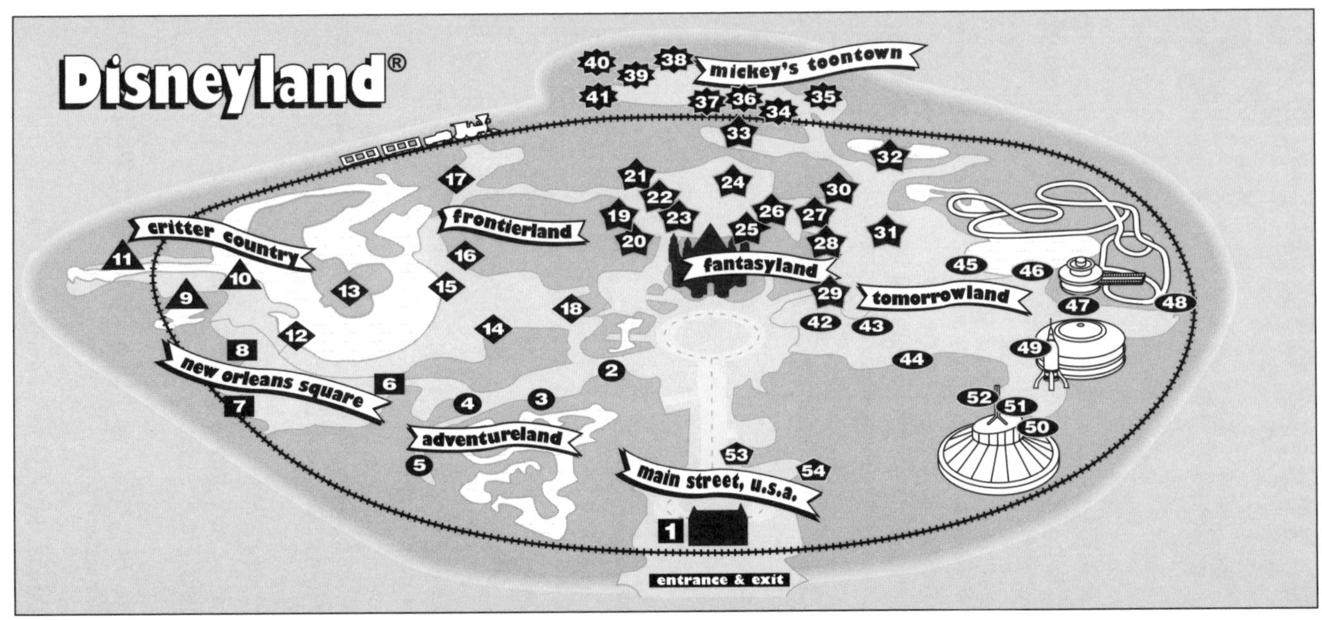
Disneyland®
mickey's toontown
critter country
frontierland
fantasyland
tomorrowland
new orleans square
adventureland
main street, u.s.a.
entrance & exit
1
2
3
4
5
6
7
8
9
10
11
12
13
14
15
16
17
18
19
20
21
22
23
24
25
26
27
28
29
30
31
32
33
34
35
36
37
38
39
40
41
42
43
44
45
46
47
48
49
50
51
52
53
54

1 Disneyland Railroad, Entrance

adventureland

2 Enchanted Tiki Room
3 Jungle Cruise
4 Tarzan's Treehouse™
5 Indiana Jones™ Adventure

new orleans square

6 Pirates of the Caribbean
7 Disneyland Railroad
8 Haunted Mansion

critter country

9 Splash Mountain
10 Davy Crockett's Explorer Canoes
11 The Many Adventures of Winnie the Pooh

frontierland

12 Rafts to Tom Sawyer Island
13 Pirate's Lair on Tom Sawyer Island
14 The Golden Horseshoe Stage
15 Mark Twain Riverboat and Sailing Ship Columbia
16 Big Thunder Mountain Railroad
17 Big Thunder Ranch
18 Frontierland Shootin' Exposition

fantasyland

19 Pinocchio's Daring Journey
20 Snow White's Scary Adventures
21 Casey Jr. Circus Train
22 King Arthur Carrousel
23 Sleeping Beauty Castle Walkthrough
24 Dumbo the Flying Elephant
25 Peter Pan's Flight
26 Mr. Toad's Wild Ride
27 Mad Tea Party
28 Alice in Wonderland
29 Pixie Hollow
30 Storybook Land Canal Boats
31 Matterhorn Bobsleds
32 "it's a small world"
33 Disney Princess Fantasy Faire

mickey's toontown

34 Disneyland Railroad
35 Roger Rabbit's Car Toon Spin
36 Goofy's Playhouse
37 Donald's Boat
38 Minnie's House
39 Mickey's House
40 Chip 'n Dale Treehouse
41 Gadget's Go Coaster

tomorrowland

42 Astro Orbitor
43 Buzz Lightyear Astro Blasters
44 Star Tours — The Adventures Continue
45 Finding Nemo Submarine Voyage
46 Disneyland Monorail
47 Autopia
48 Disneyland Railroad
49 Innoventions
50 Space Mountain
51 "Captain EO"
52 Starcade

main street, u.s.a.

53 Main Street Cinema
54 Disneyland Story... Mr. Lincoln

Clue 7: Study the right *Bobsleds* queue area for a Hidden Mickey on a coat of arms.
4 points

Clue 8: While on the ride, stay alert for a Hidden Mickey in an ice cave.
5 points

★ Now ride ***Peter Pan's Flight***.

Clue 9: At the beginning of the ride, read two names in blocks below you.
4 points for finding both

Clue 10: Look for Mickey in Big Ben.
5 points

★ Outside *Peter Pan's Flight* ...

Clue 11: Search high for a Hidden Mickey.
3 points

★ If the wait is 20 minutes or less, line up at ***Pixie Hollow Meet and Greet*** area.

Clue 12: At the end of the waiting queue, don't overlook a classic Mickey.
4 points

★ Head next to ***Buzz Lightyear Astro Blasters*** in Tomorrowland

Clue 13: Search for two Mickey continents along the entrance queue.
3 points for each one; 6 points total

Clue 14: Find two classic (three-circle) Hidden Mickeys along the entrance queue.
3 points for each one; 6 points total

Clue 15: On the ride, watch to your left for a classic Mickey on a block.
3 points

Clue 16: After you step off the ride vehicle,

search for a side-profile Mickey on the wall.
2 points

Clue 17: Find two classic Mickeys in this same mural.
2 points each

★ Return to ***Space Mountain*** during or after your FASTPASS window and walk up the entrance queue. You can skip the ride if you want; there were no Hidden Mickeys in it last time I checked.

Clue 18: Find Mickey along the entrance queue.
2 points

Clue 19: See anything on the ride vehicles?
2 points

★ Walk to ***Big Thunder Mountain Railroad*** in Frontierland.

Clue 20: While on the ride, search for three gears that form a classic Mickey.
3 points

Clue 21: Find Mickey at the exit.
3 points

★ Cross the park to Critter Country. Get a FASTPASS for *Splash Mountain* to ride later.

★ Now stroll over to ***The Many Adventures of Winnie the Pooh***.

Clue 22: Study the "Hunny Pot" vehicles for a classic Mickey.
2 points

Clue 23: Just after the ride starts, be aware of a classic Mickey in the wood.
5 points

Clue 24: Locate Mickey ears near the sleeping Pooh.
5 points

Clue 25: Look for classic Mickey circles near Heffalumps.
3 points

★ Walk to Adventureland and join the line for ***Indiana Jones Adventure***.

Clue 26: Study the walls of the Standby queue for Mickey's "initials."
4 points

Clue 27: In the circular room with the rope you can pull on, search for a stone disk (propped upright) with a tiny classic Mickey.
5 points

Clue 28: Now look up for another classic Mickey in the same room.
3 points

Clue 29: Find a large classic Mickey in the room with the video screen.
4 points

Clue 30: Toward the end of the video room, look up and say hi to Eeyore!
5 points

Clue 31: When you leave the video room, peer into an office to spot Mickey.
3 points

Clue 32: After the ride starts, gaze up into Mara's huge face for a classic Mickey.
3 points

Clue 33: When your vehicle enters the Mummy Room, find a Mickey Mouse hat.
5 points

★ Wander over to New Orleans Square and hop on ***Pirates of the Caribbean***.

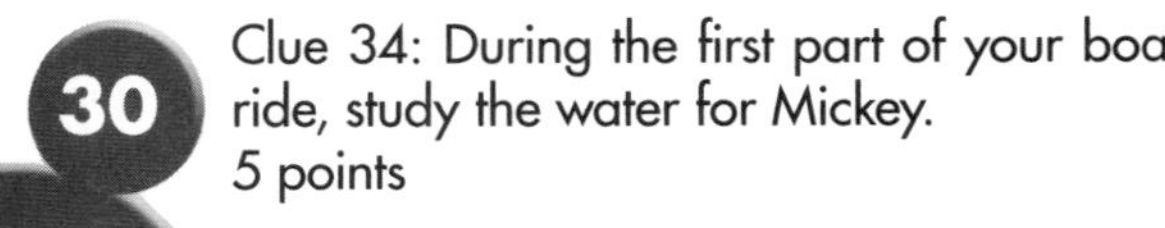

Clue 34: During the first part of your boat ride, study the water for Mickey.
5 points

Clue 35: Stay alert for Mickey on a chair by a bed.
4 points

Clue 36: After you pass the skeleton in bed, look back for an image of Goofy.
5 points

Clue 37: In the first fight scene, spot a classic Mickey on a wall.
5 points

Clue 38: After you exit the boat, look around for a classic Mickey on a door.
2 points

★ Turn left at the exit to enjoy ***Haunted Mansion***.

Clue 39: Look high along the mansion walls for a Hidden Mickey.
3 points

Clue 40: Search for Mickey in the wallpaper.
3 points

Clue 41: While on the ride, can you find Donald Duck?
4 points

Clue 42: As you ride, keep alert for plates and saucers.
3 points

Clue 43: In the attic, look for a clock with a Hidden Mickey.
5 points

★ Mosey on over to ***The Golden Horseshoe***. You can order a counter-service lunch and, if the timing is right, catch a great show on its stage (check your Times Guide).

Clue 44: Check around the stage for a classic Mickey.
3 points

★ Ride ***Mark Twain Riverboat*** or ***Sailing Ship Columbia***.

Clue 45: While on the boat, scour the river for a classic Mickey in the water.
3 points

Clue 46: Seek out the ***Mark Twain Riverboat*** (if you haven't already). Concentrate on the front of the boat to spot a Hidden Mickey.
2 points

Clue 47: Search for Mickey Mouse in a painting near the *Mark Twain Riverboat* loading dock.
5 points

★ Float on the ***Raft to Tom Sawyer Island***.

Clue 48: On *Tom Sawyer Island,* seek out a cavern entrance with a classic Mickey.
3 points

Clue 49: Climb up into the first treehouse you find and look outside and down for a classic Mickey.
4 points

★ Return by raft to Frontierland. Turn right and walk to the ***Briar Patch*** store in Critter Country (near *Splash Mountain*).

Clue 50: Look inside the store for a Hidden Mickey.
3 points

★ Ride ***Splash Mountain*** with your FASTPASS.

Clue 51: Check out the outside entrance queue for a tiny Mickey.
5 points

Clue 52: Search for a classic Mickey along the inside queue.
3 points

Clue 53: While on the ride, stay alert for a picture of Mickey on the wall.
4 points

★ Stroll to ***Big Thunder Ranch***.

Clue 54: Spot a Hidden Mickey near the entrance.
4 points

Clue 55: Don't miss Mickey atop a big pile!
4 points

★ Cross the central hub to Tomorrowland. Get a FASTPASS for *Star Tours: The Adventures Continue* to enjoy later. Then walk along the entrance queue for ***Autopia***.

Clue 56: Find a classic Mickey on the cars.
3 points

★ Make time in your schedule for the ***afternoon parade***. (Note: The parade floats change from time to time but usually include Hidden Mickeys in their decoration). The antique Grand Marshal automobile sometimes leads the parade.

Clue 57: Search this antique car for several Hidden Mickeys.
5 bonus points for finding three or more

★ In Adventureland, line up for the ***Jungle Cruise***.

Clue 58: Search the side of the river for Donald Duck's face on a native.
4 points

★ If you're up for a mild climb through an imaginative tree, check out ***Tarzan's Treehouse*** in Adventureland.

Clue 59: Study the room with the ship's wheel for a Hidden Mickey near the floor.
3 points

Clue 60: In this same room, look for a Hidden Mickey on the wall.
3 points

Clue 61: Along your walk through the tree, two characters from *Beauty and the Beast* make an appearance.
4 points for finding both

Clue 62: Watch for a classic Mickey made of "drums."
3 points

★ Stroll toward the ***Enchanted Tiki Room***.

Clue 63: Observe the shields outside near the exit to find a classic Mickey.
3 points

★ Walk back across the central hub and through Fantasyland to ***Mickey's Toontown*** (or hop on the *Disneyland Railroad* train at New Orleans Square and get off in Toontown).

(Note: You'll find many Mickey shapes throughout Toontown. I don't include the larger, more obvious Mickey images as Hidden Mickeys; they're more properly designated "décor" Mickeys.)

Clue 64: Look for Mickey near the entrance to Mickey's Toontown.
2 points

★ Get in line for ***Gadget's Go Coaster***. The Hidden Mickeys here are along the queue. You can skip the actual ride if you want; just ask to exit when you reach the loading area.

Clue 65: Stay alert for at least three rock classic Mickeys in the queue walls.
3 points each; 9 points total

Clue 66: Gaze around the vehicle loading area for a Hidden Mickey.
4 points

★ Stroll over to ***Mickey's House***.

Clue 67: See anything in his front door?
1 point

Clue 68: Glance down for Mickey.
1 point

Clues 69 and 70: Look inside a glass-fronted bookcase for several Hidden Mickeys.
3 points for one on each of two books

Clue 71: Stare at other books in the first room.
3 points

Clues 72 and 73: In the piano room, search for two Hidden Mickeys in a bookcase.
2 points each; 4 points total

Clue 74: Find classic Mickeys in the piano.
2 points total

Clue 75: Something's atop the piano.
2 points

Clue 76: Pay attention to a special mirror inside Mickey's Movie Barn (the room in *Mickey's House* where you wait to meet Mickey in person).
4 points

Clue 77: Also in Mickey's Movie Barn, watch the count-down screen.
4 points

Clue 78: Once outside, admire Mickey's car and find a Hidden Mickey.
3 points

Clue 79: Search for Mickey on a lamp.
3 points

★ Saunter over to ***Minnie's House***.

Clue 80: Mickey is hiding in the first room inside.
3 points

Clue 81: Mickey is also hiding in Minnie's kitchen.
2 points

★ Search for Mickey outside *Minnie's House.*

Clue 82: Look near the big blue doors.
5 points

★ Locate the ***telephone hut*** near *Minnie's House.*

Clue 83: Find Mickey in the small building with the telephones.
2 points

★ If you're in Mickey's Toontown when ***Clarabelle's Frozen Yogurt*** closes, look around for a Hidden Mickey. (Ask a Cast Member about closing time; you may need to return later.)

Clue 84: At closing, a Hidden Mickey appears.
2 points

Clue 85: Find two more at the ***Post Office***.
4 points for finding both

Clue 86: Ring the doorbell at the ***Toontown Fire Department*** and watch for a Hidden Mickey.
5 points

★ Walk back to Fantasyland and queue up to ride ***Alice in Wonderland***.

Clue 87: On the ride, search for a classic Mickey in red paint.
4 points

★ Get in line for ***Mr. Toad's Wild Ride***.

Clue 88: Find a tiny Mickey along the entrance queue.
4 points

Clue 89: At the beginning of the ride, stare at a right-hand door for a tiny dark Mickey in the door's stained glass.
5 points

Clue 90: Search for Mickey in beer foam.
4 points

★ Go to ***Snow White's Scary Adventures***.

Clue 91: Find Mickey at the loading dock.
3 points

Clue 92: On the ride, watch for a classic Mickey on an animal.
3 points

★ Go next door to ***Pinocchio's Daring Journey***.

Clue 93: Watch the floor for a yellow Hidden Mickey.
4 points

Clue 94: Check the popcorn stand on your right for a classic Mickey.
4 points

Clue 95: Look for a Hidden Mickey near a ship.
5 points

★ Amble over to ***Casey Jr. Circus Train***.

Clue 96: Examine the conductor's cabin for Mickey.
3 points

★ Walk to the ***Storybook Land Canal Boats*** ride and look for the boat named "Flora." If you don't see it right away, ride another boat and look for "Flora" after you exit.

Clue 97: Study the "Flora" boat for a Hidden Mickey.
4 points

Clue 98: While on the boat ride, search for a Hidden Mickey above a village.
3 points

★ Relax on a gentle boat ride at ***"it's a small world."***

Clue 99: Look for Mickey along the entrance queue.
3 points

Clue 100: Stay alert for Hidden Characters.
5 points for spotting five or more

Clue 101: Watch the ceiling for a Hidden Mickey.
3 points

★ Stroll over to ***King Arthur Carrousel***. Find the Hidden Mickeys from outside the Carrousel first, then ride if you wish.

Clue 102: Check out the horses for Hidden Mickeys.
2 points each; 4 points total

★ Cross Fantasyland to the ***Mad Hatter*** shop, not far from the *Mad Tea Party* attraction.

Clue 103: Search around inside the shop for a Hidden cat.
5 points

Clue 104: Spot Hidden Mickeys outside the shop.
2 points each for two Hidden Mickeys

★ Back near Sleeping Beauty Castle, locate the ***Castle Heraldry Shoppe***.

Clue 105: Find two Hidden Mickeys outside the store.
5 points for finding both

★ Walk to Tomorrowland. Go to *Finding Nemo Submarine Voyage* and then look for the Monorail exit to find the ***elevator for the Disneyland Monorail***.

Clue 106: Search for Mickey near the elevator.
5 points

★ Ask a Cast Member for permission to enter the ***Marine Observation Outpost*** at the right side of the *Finding Nemo Submarine Voyage* entrance queue.

Clue 107: Look around inside for a Hidden Mickey.
4 points

★ During or after your FASTPASS window, check into ***Star Tours—The Adventures Continue***.

Clue 108: Along the entrance queue, spot a Hidden Mickey near C-3PO.
3 points

Clue 109: Now wait for a shadow Hidden

Mickey in a video on a wall display along the entrance queue.
4 points

Clue 110: Next, study the entrance queue luggage scanner for Mickey and other Disney characters and images.
5 points total for finding Mickey and two or more other Disney images

★ Go to ***Innoventions***.

Clue 111: Just after you enter the building, check out Tom Morrow for a Hidden Mickey. (Note: Tom Morrow may not be on display when you visit).
4 bonus points

★ Check your Times Guide or ask a Cast Member when the next *ASIMO* show is scheduled and factor it into your itinerary. Now enjoy the ***Dream Home***, and spot a few Hidden Mickeys.

Clue 112: Don't miss Mickey at the front door!
3 points

Clue 113: Search outside and just inside the front door.
3 points total for finding Mickey in both areas

Clue 114: Look down for Mickey as you walk through the *Dream Home*.
2 points

Clue 115: Find two images of Mickey in the boy's bedroom.
4 points for finding both

Clue 116: Check the inside murals for classic Mickeys.
4 points

Clue 117: Study a wall in the ***ASIMO robot show area*** for a Hidden Mickey.
3 points

Clue 118: Find Mickey near the computer in the *ASIMO show* area.
3 points

Clue 119: Watch the *ASIMO show* video for a Hidden Mickey.
4 points

★ Exit *Innoventions*.

Clue 120: Study the rotating murals on the outside walls for two Hidden Mickeys.
4 points for spotting both

Clue 121: Now study the rotating murals for another Hidden Character.
4 points

★ Enjoy ***"Captain EO."***

Clue 122: Observe Captain EO's ship.
3 points

★ Walk to the rear of Tomorrowland to ***Redd Rockett's Pizza Port*** to find another Hidden Mickey and catch a bite to eat if you wish.

Clue 123: Search around inside the restaurant for a Hidden Mickey.
3 points

★ Retrace your steps to ***The Star Trader*** shop (not far from *Star Tours*).

Clue 124: Glance inside the store for small classic Mickeys.
2 points

★ Walk ***toward the central hub***.

Clue 125: Study the spheres of the *Astro Orbitor*.
2 points

★ Cross the central hub to the ***walkway to Frontierland***.

Clue 126: Look for a Hidden Mickey along the entrance walkway to Frontierland.
3 points

★ Stop in at the ***Frontierland Shootin' Exposition***.

Clue 127: Spot a Hidden Mickey toward the front of the shootin' area.
3 points

★ Enter the ***Pioneer Mercantile*** shop.

Clue 128: Examine the wall for Mickey.
3 points

Clue 129: Locate Mickey near a cashier.
3 points

★ Walk to the ***Rancho del Zocalo Restaurante***.

Clue 130: Search inside the restaurant for a classic Mickey in wood.
4 points

★ Go left to the ***River Belle Terrace*** restaurant.

Clue 131: Find a Hidden Mickey in the restaurant.
3 points

★ Return to ***Main Street, U.S.A.***

Clue 132: Check inside the ***Plaza Inn*** restaurant.
3 points

★ Enter the ***Photo Supply Company***.

Clue 133: Look for Mickey on a camera.
3 points

★ Stand outside the ***Silhouette Studio***.

Clue 134: Spot a Hidden Mickey in a display window.
4 points

Clue 135: Find a Hidden Mickey outside on a ***fruit cart***.
4 points

★ Enter the ***Market House***.

Clue 136: Search the wall for a Hidden Mickey.
3 points

★ Stroll down Main Street to ***Main Street Cinema***. Walk inside.

Clue 137: Look around for some Hidden Mickeys.
3 points

Clue 138: Outside Main Street Cinema, search for two Hidden Mickeys.
2 points each; 4 points total

★ Find more Mickeys at the ***Main Street Magic Shop***.

Clue 139: Spot Mickey on a display shelf.
3 points

Clue 140: Locate a classic Mickey outside the shop.
3 points

★ Walk toward the Castle to the ***Penny Arcade***.

Clue 141: Don't miss the small Hidden Mickey on a game machine inside the Penny Arcade!
4 points

★ Enter the ***Gibson Girl Ice Cream Parlor***.

Clue 142: Look up for a Hidden Mickey.
2 points

★ Walk over to the ***Blue Ribbon Bakery***.

Clue 143: Study the walls inside the bakery for a Hidden Mickey.
3 points

★ Stroll to the ***Emporium*** store.

Clue 144: Admire the outside window displays for classic Mickeys.
2 points total for one or more

★ Walk to the ***Main Street Station of the Disneyland Railroad***.

Clue 145: Wait for the trains and study their forward sections for Hidden Mickeys.
5 points total for one or more

★ Watch the ***Fantasmic!*** show for a Hidden Mickey.

Clue 146: Be alert for a Hidden Mickey on the water screen.
5 points

★ Don't miss the nighttime ***fireworks show***!

Clue 147: Watch the sky during the fireworks show for a Hidden Mickey.
5 points

★ Exit Disneyland Park.

Clue 148: In the ***entrance plaza***, look for Mickey at your feet.
3 points

Clue 149: Now spot Mickey at the tops and bottoms of some of the poles.
4 points for spotting Mickey in both places

Total Points for Disneyland Park =

How'd You Do?

Up to 194 points – Bronze
195 to 387 points – Silver
388 points and over – Gold
485 points – Perfect Score

(If you earned bonus points by spotting Hidden Mickeys on the Grand Marshal's car during the afternoon parade or in *Innoventions*, you may have done even better.)

**Caution:
Don't peek at this section unless you really want help!**

HINTS HINTS HINTS HINTS HINTS HINTS HINTS HINTS HINTS HINTS HINTS HINTS HINTS

Security Bag Check Area

Hint 1: Various pictures of characters from *The Lion King* hang above you. On the picture with the warning "Hold On To Your Gear!" a small key chain flies through the air behind Timon and Pumbaa on a roller coaster. A tiny black classic Mickey is on the blue part of the key chain. (You may need to wander around the security area to find the picture.)

Hint 2: On the sign warning "Let The Cubs Decide If They Want To Ride," a small white classic Mickey is above the word "Cubs" on a blue ride vehicle occupied by Timon and Pumbaa.

Hint 3: Timon and Pumbaa are wearing Mickey ears on the sign that says "Keep Arms, Hooves, Tusks and Tails inside the Vehicle" as well as on the sign that says "Be Aware, It's a Jungle Out There!"

Hint 4: In a sign that says "Stay On Your

Feet, It's Not a Seat," Timon wears Mickey ears and another Mickey hat flies through the air. In the sign that says "Paws Behind the Line," Mickey ears fly through the air above a cloud near a pink castle.

Entrance

Hint 5: As soon as you enter Disneyland, turn around and spot the classic Mickey speaker grid on the utility box next to the entrance turnstile. (Note: The ticket attendant may be blocking your view.)

Fantasyland

- *Matterhorn Bobsleds*

Hint 6: A large black classic Mickey hole hides in the side of the Matterhorn mountain. You can see it from various vantage points in Tomorrowland.

Hint 7: A tiny black classic Mickey is in the middle of a red and white coat of arms at the rear of the right queue. The Mickey is on a red triangle at the bottom of a white pole.

Hint 8: To your left during the first part of the ride, on the floor of the first ice cave, where you will see expedition equipment and glowing crystals, a rope between the ice crystals and the crates is coiled into a classic Mickey. (Note: This Hidden Mickey comes and goes.)

- *Peter Pan's Flight*

Hint 9: As you walk through the entrance queue, lean over the rail and look into the first scene (the bedroom) of the ride. Alphabet blocks are stacked and scattered on the floor. On the ride, as your vehicle soars over the bedroom, look down at the blocks and find these words: "DISNEY" (spelled as "D13NEY") and "PETER PAN." (Cast Members may change these blocks around at times).

Hint 10: As you fly over London, a side-view Mickey silhouette hides in a top window on the left side of Big Ben. Look back

at the window as you pass by the clock tower.

Hint 11: Inside a high window to the left of the entrance to the attraction, classic Mickeys are on the bottom of a plush bear's paws. The paws are at the lower right, next to the window curtain.

- *Pixie Hollow Meet and Greet*

Hint 12: At the end of the *Pixie Hollow* waiting queue is a signpost that reads "Fairies Welcome." A classic Mickey is carved out of bark on the front of the signpost, near the bottom.

Tomorrowland

- *Buzz Lightyear Astro Blasters*

Hint 13: As soon as you enter the building, look for two "Ska-densii" planets with side-profile "continent" Mickeys along the right side wall.

Hint 14: Two upside-down classic Mickeys appear in the large "Planets of the Galactic Alliance" mural on the wall of the entrance queue. One is located at about the "10 o'clock" position in the planet named K'lifooel'ch; it is made of small green spheres. The other is made of white spheres and hides on the right side of the mural above the words "K'tleendon Kan Cluster."

Hint 15: A classic Mickey is etched on a block in the first show room to the left of the vehicle, just past a large rotating wheel and left of a row of target batteries

Hint 16: A side-profile Mickey hides on a "Ska-densii" planet's continent on a right wall mural across from the photo viewing area. If it looks familiar, it's because you see the same Hidden Mickeys (as well as the two below) on an entrance-queue mural.

Hint 17: On this same mural on the right wall along the inside exit, a classic Mickey

lies along the outer edge of the K'lifooel'ch planet of spheres at about the "10 o'clock" location (other classic Mickey spheres are in this planet) and an upside-down classic Mickey is formed by three white spheres at the middle right of the mural, above the words "K'tleendon Kan Cluster."

- *Space Mountain*

Hint 18: Mickey ears appear on the right side of the safety video in which you're asked to place "loose possessions in the storage pouch in front of you."

Hint 19: The speakers on the back of the ride vehicle seats form classic Mickeys.

Frontierland

- *Big Thunder Mountain Railroad*

Hint 20: As you start to climb the second hill, look to your left, near the bottom of the hill, for three gears that form a large, upside-down classic Mickey.

Hint 21: On your right as you exit, the highest three green lobes in the cactus garden form an oval classic Mickey. At times, other collections of cactus lobes may also form Mickeys.

Critter Country

- *The Many Adventures of Winnie the Pooh*

Hint 22: The back and lower legs of the "Heffabee" on top of each ride vehicle form an upside-down classic Mickey.

Hint 23: In the first part of the entrance tunnel, a small classic Hidden Mickey hides on the bark of a round tree trunk that you reach just before you get to the wall covered with colorful leaves. He's to the right of your vehicle, at about eye level.

Hint 24: In the scene to the left of your vehicle where Winnie the Pooh is sleeping and begins to float in the air, you can spot

Mickey ears on the upper shelf of a desk to the far side of Pooh, in the corner of the room.

Hint 25: Near the end of the ride, there is a Heffalump collage on your right. Look in the bottom right-hand corner for an upside down classic Mickey.

Adventureland

- *Indiana Jones Adventure*

Hint 26: Across from the first drinking fountains in the inside Standby queue, Mickey's initials, "M M" in Mara script, are on the left wall, just above a horizontal crack in the wall.

Hint 27: On the side of a bamboo structure just opposite the hanging rope, a large painted stone disk has a tiny classic Hidden Mickey symbol on the lower right edge of the outer circle of symbols.

Hint 28: On the ceiling, Mara's giant nose is a classic Mickey.

Hint 29: When you enter the room showing the video on a screen, study the left wall for a large classic Hidden Mickey between the last two lights on the wall.

Hint 30: *Indiana Jones Adventure* was built over a previous Eeyore (cast) parking lot. As a tribute to the past, an original white parking sign shaped as Eeyore was placed in the video room, high up in the rafters. To spot it, go to the end of the video room, turn around, and look up to the left of the projector. If you can't find it, ask a nearby Cast Member for help.

Hint 31: In an office just past the video room, Mickey and Minnie Mouse are pictured on a partially visible magazine page. The magazine is on a desktop.

Hint 32: Shortly after the ride starts, look at Mara's face for a (not quite perfect) classic

Mickey formed by the curves of the nostrils and the oval depression just below the middle of the nose.

Hint 33: As soon as your vehicle turns a corner and enters the Mummy Room, look left for a skeleton wearing a Mickey Mouse hat. Let's hope the hat stays put!

New Orleans Square

- *Pirates of the Caribbean*

Hint 34: As you drift past the Blue Bayou Restaurant seating area, a classic Mickey appears in the water to the right of your boat. It's formed by the last set of three lily pads that you pass before you enter the caverns.

Hint 35: To the left of your boat, a classic Mickey hides on the upper back of the chair near the pirate skeleton in bed.

Hint 36: Just after you float by the skeleton in bed on your left, look back at the ceiling of the cavern for a large rock that juts out over the water above you. The shape of the rock resembles Goofy.

Hint 37: In the first battle scene, there are three cannonball impact craters on the upper part of the fort wall on the right side of your boat. This crater classic Mickey is below the middle cannon and best seen if you turn around to view it as you are passing by the fort.

Hint 38: On the right side as you exit, and before you reach the street outside, a classic Mickey-shaped lock adorns a back door to the Pieces of Eight shop.

- *Haunted Mansion*

Hint 39: As soon as you walk through the front door along the entrance queue, go to any of the candlestick holders on the wall and, with your back to the wall, look up from underneath to spot a classic Mickey effect.

Hint 40: Large circles form classic Mickeys in the wallpaper of the Art Gallery after you exit the Stretching Room.

Hint 41: As you pass by the "endless hallway," check out the back of the purple chair for an abstract Donald Duck. Near the top of the chair, you can see his cap, which sits above his distorted eyes, face and bill. (Note that the chair may change locations at times).

Hint 42: During the Ballroom scene, look down at the place settings near the center of the dining table. You'll see two small saucers and one larger plate forming a classic Mickey. The Cast Members move this Hidden Mickey around at times.

Hint 43: After the ballroom scene, look to the right as soon as you enter the attic. Find the clock on a bureau to the right of the round portrait of a bride and groom and just to the right of a bright orange and blue lamp. A brown classic Mickey hides behind the pendulum of the clock.

Frontierland

- *The Golden Horseshoe*

Hint 44: Walk toward the front of the stage and find a vent grate in the center of the lower front wall. Start at the lower right hole in the grate. Then look up and diagonally left one hole to spot a classic Mickey hole in the grate.

- *Mark Twain Riverboat/Sailing Ship Columbia*

Hint 45: While boating the Rivers of America, look out for three boulders in the water that form a classic Mickey. These boulders are on the right side of your vessel near the shore of *Tom Sawyer Island* and across the river from an Indian scene.

Hint 46: Study the metal grillwork between the smokestacks and high above the *Mark*

Twain riverboat's prow for a sideways classic Mickey.

Hint 47: To the right of the entrance for the *Mark Twain Riverboat* is a "Shipping Office." A painting advertising river excursions on the *Mark Twain* hangs on an "office" wall. In the painting, Mickey Mouse is one of the passengers on the lowest deck.

- *Tom Sawyer Island*

Hint 48: As you exit the raft onto the island, turn left and look above the first cavern entrance you encounter. A classic Mickey depression is in the rock over the entrance.

Hint 49: Climb into the treehouse and look toward the Rivers of America. A classic, smiling Mickey is etched onto the top horizontal cover of a short chimney.

- *Briar Patch store*

Hint 50: A classic Mickey made from heads of lettuce sits on an upper shelf over the front window inside the Briar Patch store.

Critter Country

- *Splash Mountain*

Hint 51: A tiny classic Mickey is formed of indentations in a protruding knot on a post at the beginning of the outside Standby entrance queue. Mickey is on the post just below the *Splash Mountain* Warning sign. You can also spot this Mickey as you exit *Haunted Mansion.*

Hint 52: As you enter the inside part of the entrance queue, look along the left side for a three-gear classic Mickey.

Hint 53: Near the end of the ride, after the big drop, you can spot a framed photo of Mickey Mouse (riding in a *Splash Mountain* log) on the upper wall, to the left of your log.

Frontierland

- *Big Thunder Ranch*

Hint 54: At the entrance/exit, a classic Mickey formed by holes in the wood is under the soap dispenser next to the hand-washing station.

Hint 55: Behind a fence to the left of the Ranch Cabin, you can see a huge pile of leaves and horseshoes. Three horseshoes at the upper right of the pile are positioned to resemble a classic Mickey.

Tomorrowland

- *Autopia*

Hint 56: A black classic Mickey hides in the upper right corner of the car license plates.

Afternoon Parade

Hint 57: On this attractive replica of an antique touring car, classic Mickeys adorn the tires, the front bumper, the hood ornament, nuts at the side of the front windshield, the tread on the spare tire on the rear of the car, and the brackets holding the spare tire in place.

Adventureland

- *Jungle Cruise*

Hint 58: Along the left side of the boat, be alert for menacing natives with spears. The next to last isolated native of the group wears a Donald mask.

- *Tarzan's Treehouse*

Hint 59: Look for a trunk on the floor near the ship's wheel. The gold metal plate where the trunk's keyhole is located includes a classic Mickey made of round metal pieces. One of them encircles the keyhole.

Hint 60: Behind the ship's wheel, the far right curtain knobs at the right rear of the room form a classic Mickey. The curtain knobs directly to the left resemble a classic Mickey as well.

Hint 61: Pots that resemble Mrs. Potts and Chip from the *Beauty and the Beast* movie sit alongside the trail near the end.

Hint 62: Toward the end of the trail, three hollow drums (or pots) are arranged to form a classic Mickey.

-Enchanted Tiki Room

Hint 63: Four shields hang over the *Enchanted Tiki Room* exit. A classic Mickey with two smiley faces for "ears" hides near the bottom of the left shield.

Mickey's Toontown

- Near the entrance

Hint 64: A white silhouette of Mickey's face and ears, seen from the front, adorns the "Order of Mouse" seal on the overhead bridge to the left of the "Welcome to Mickey's Toontown" sign.

- Gadget's Go Coaster

Hint 65: These classic Mickeys aren't perfectly proportional, but they seem purposeful:

- The first is at the first turn to the left in the entrance queue.
- The second is across from a bonsai tree and before the last right turn.
- The third is a somewhat distorted classic Mickey, facing sideways, at the end of the wall on the left and about 20 feet before the boarding area.

Hint 66: Inside the loading area, turn around and locate the only blueprint on the rear wall. A partial drawing of Mickey Mouse is on the right side of the blueprint. Under Mickey are the words "DOG & PONY FOR MICKEY AT 4 PM."

- Approaching, in, and exiting Mickey's House

Hint 67: The window in Mickey's green front door is a partial classic-Mickey shape.

Hint 68: The welcome mat at Mickey's front door is shaped like a classic Mickey.

Hint 69: As you enter the first room, stop by the green, glass-fronted bookcase. The top of the spine of the book "2001: A Mouse Odyssey" is decorated with two gold classic Mickeys.

Hint 70: In the same bookcase, find the orange book, "See You Next Squeak." At the bottom of the spine, the publisher's logo is a classic Mickey enclosed in a square.

Hint 71: At the left side of the first room, the bottom of the spine of the blue book entitled "My Fair Mouse" sports a classic Mickey.

Hint 72: Just as you enter the piano room, study the bookcase on the right side. The book "My Life with Walt" has a pink classic Mickey at the top of the spine.

Hint 73: In the same bookcase, locate the book "Pluto's Republic." To its immediate left, a thin green book has a yellow classic Mickey at the top of its spine.

Hint 74: Most of the holes in the paper for the player piano are classic Mickeys.

Hint 75: The weight for the metronome on top of the player piano is a classic Mickey.

Hint 76: There is a mirror on the right side inside Mickey's Movie Barn. Stare at it and wait awhile. Mickey Mouse's head will appear.

Hint 77: Also in Mickey's Movie Barn (and before you meet Mickey Mouse in person), a classic Mickey appears around

the countdown numbers on the screen before the film starts.

Hint 78: Mickey's red car sits outside his house in his driveway. The car's hubcaps sport white classic Mickeys.

Hint 79: Outside the exit from *Mickey's House*, classic Mickeys hide in the decorative ironwork on a lamp sitting on a short post.

- In and outside of Minnie's House

Hint 80: Inside *Minnie's House*, you'll see a row of books in the first room on the right side. Look for a pink book next to a book entitled "Little Mouse on the Prairie." The mark at the top of the pink book's spine is a classic Mickey combined with the medical symbol for "female." (Could the symbol be a Hidden Minnie?)

Hint 81: Inside the refrigerator in Minnie's kitchen, a bottle of cheese relish on the second shelf in the door has a red classic Mickey "brand mark" at the top of the label.

Hint 82: To the right of the large blue doors that lead backstage near *Minnie's House*, a small opening leads to a "Cast Members Only" entrance and exit. Walk into this opening and look left to spot a blue rock classic Mickey in the wall.

Hint 83: A classic Mickey hole is in middle of the telephone dials.

- Clarabelle's Frozen Yogurt

Hint 84: A shutter is pulled down when Clarabelle's Frozen Yogurt closes for business. A white classic Mickey marking is on the left side of the shutter.

- Toontown Post Office

Hint 85: At the Post Office, Mickey is on the postage stamp on the letter above the entrance, and you'll find a side profile of

Mickey (along with five other characters) inside the Post Office on the wall-mounted mailboxes.

- *Toontown Fire Department*

Hint 86: When you ring the doorbell at the Fire Department, move back quickly to spot the Dalmatian puppy who looks out of an upper middle window for a few seconds. A sideways classic Mickey made of black spots is on his upper forehead.

Fantasyland

- *Alice in Wonderland*

Hint 87: When the cards are "painting the roses red," look on the ground under the tree to the left for a slightly distorted classic Mickey. It's on a third-level ledge under the right hand with the paint brush, just to the left of a green heart.

- *Mr. Toad's Wild Ride*

Hint 88: On the large statue of Mr. Toad, to the left of the inside entrance queue, a tiny red classic Mickey is at the lower part of his right cornea (above the white of the eye). It's in the left eye as you face the statue.

Hint 89: At the beginning of the ride, on the third set of doors that your car drives through, you'll see the head and ears of a tiny dark Mickey, in the lower left panel in the bottom left-most triangle of stained glass. This Mickey is hard to spot!

Hint 90: In Winky's Pub, about halfway through the ride, an upside-down classic Mickey appears in the foam in the top left corner of the left mug (as you face the scene) above Winky's hand.

- *Snow White's Scary Adventures*

Hint 91: A somewhat distorted three-quarter side-profile Mickey is formed by bushes in the mural directly in front of your ride vehicle at the loading area. Look at the right end of the row of green bushes just past the rocky hill and to the left of the blue stream. Mickey is looking to the left.

Hint 92: Early on in the ride, look for the green turtle climbing the stairs to the left of your ride vehicle. The large circle on the left side of the turtle's shell forms the "head" of a three-circle classic Mickey.

- *Pinocchio's Daring Journey*

Hint 93: When your vehicle enters the Pleasure Island room, study the ground in front of the popcorn stand on your right. Some "spilled" popcorn makes a classic Hidden Mickey.

Hint 94: Look back at the left side window in the popcorn stand for an upside-down classic Mickey in the popcorn, about one-third the way up in the window.

Hint 95: Near the end of the ride a big case holds a model ship. The middle of the top frame of the case is decorated with a wooden classic Mickey.

- *Casey Jr. Circus Train*

Hint 96: In the middle of the control panel at the front of the conductor's cabin, three round dials form a classic Mickey. You can spot this Mickey from the entrance area, so you can skip the ride if you want.

- *Storybook Land Canal Boats*

Hint 97: On the rear side of the "Flora" boat, a small purple classic Mickey is hiding in the flower design.

Hint 98: The pumpkin carriage on the upper road approaching Cinderella's village simulates an upside-down classic Mickey. The pumpkin is the "head" and the side wheels are the "ears."

- *"it's a small world"*

Hint 99: Three circular control towers topped by umbrellas overlook the entrance queue. The center tower is larger than the

other two, so together they form a classic Mickey.

Hint 100: Disney characters appear alongside your tour boat. Look for Alice in Wonderland, Cinderella, Pinocchio, Ariel, Nemo, Woody and Jessie, Lilo and Stitch, and others.

Hint 101: In the last room of the ride, shadows from the last set of small balloons that move up and down form classic Mickeys at times to the left of your boat.

- King Arthur Carrousel

Hint 102: Find the golden horse, Jingles. Classic Mickeys made of gemstones are on the front and back of the horse. These classic Mickeys aren't perfectly proportioned and the "ears" and "head" don't touch, but they seem purposeful.

- Mad Hatter shop

Hint 103: Every few minutes, a faint image of the Cheshire Cat appears in the mirror above the check-out area.

Hint 104: A Mickey hat with ears hides at one corner of each of two outdoor signs for the shop.

- Castle Heraldry Shoppe

Hint 105: Near the Castle Heraldry Shoppe, a classic Mickey is in the bottom center of the painted scroll trim at the edges of an outdoor mailbox. Also look for the classic Mickeys wearing "Mickey's Sorcerer's Hat." They're repeated at the end of some of the branches in the scrollwork at the top and bottom.

Tomorrowland

- Near Finding Nemo & the Monorail exit

Hint 106: A classic Mickey impression is in the rock wall about one foot off the floor and between two separated handrails.

- *Finding Nemo: Marine Observation Outpost*

Hint 107: Look for the lockers on the left front wall inside the Marine Observation Outpost. You can spot Sorcerer Mickey inside locker No. 105. He's on the clothing that's under a pair of sunglasses.

- *Star Tours—The Adventures Continue*

Hint 108: Circles create a Mickey hat with ears on the upper part of the control panel behind C-3PO's head.

Hint 109: In a wall display along the entrance queue, the silhouette of R2-D2 appears several times in a continuous video loop of moving shadow figures. At one point, R2-D2 sprouts satellite ears that rotate into round "Mickey ears" for a few seconds.

Hint 110: Along the entrance queue, a robot watches a continuous scan of luggage moving along a conveyor belt. You can spot images of a plush Mickey Mouse and a plush Goofy, along with images of Buzz Lightyear, Aladdin's lamp, a Sorcerer Mickey hat, a Mr. Incredible shirt, Madame Leota's crystal ball, and others.

- *Innoventions*

Hint 111: Look down to Tom Morrow's shoelaces; they're covered with pink classic Mickeys.

Hint 112: A shadow of Mickey runs across the large window near the front door, just outside the *Dream Home*.

Hint 113: Classic Mickeys are in the middle of the railings just outside and inside the front door.

Hint 114: Classic Mickeys are among the circles in the main hallway carpet leading toward the kitchen.

Hint 115: Side-profile Mickey-shaped bookends support the books on a middle shelf. Nearby on the same shelf is a small picture of Mickey kicking a soccer ball.

Hint 116: On a wall mural inside *Innoventions* but just outside the *Dream Home,* several classic Mickeys are formed by grapes at the lower part of vertical vines.

Hint 117: A small black classic Mickey hides in the lower part of a painting on a wall of the *ASIMO* stage.

Hint 118: On the *ASIMO show* stage, a Mickey doll is on the desk next to the computer monitor.

Hint 119: When the lady talks to her husband over the videophone, you can see a side view of Mickey on the wall behind the husband.

Hint 120: Among items in the Entertainment section of the rotating wall murals outside is a black classic Mickey on a video monitor. In another mural, a large classic Mickey is on a blue wall, partially hidden behind a red monitor screen.

Hint 121: Also on the outside rotating murals, find a globe on a pedestal. Goofy's long nose pokes out from the eastern side of the land mass at the top. He's looking to the right.

- *"Captain EO"*

Hint 122: In the movie, the three lower thrusters on the back of Captain EO's spaceship form a classic Hidden Mickey.

- *Redd Rockett's Pizza Port*

Hint 123: On a wall inside the restaurant, groups of circles decorate a poster entitled "Adventure Thru Inner Space." The circles in the middle right of the poster approximate a classic Mickey.

- *The Star Trader*

Hint 124: Classic Mickey holes are in some of the shop's upright merchandise display poles.

- Astro Orbitor

Hint 125: The moving spheres above the *Astro Orbitor* occasionally form classic Mickeys.

Frontierland

- Entrance walkway from the central hub

Hint 126: A cannon sits to the right, just past the Frontierland sign on the entrance walkway from the central hub. In the tongue behind the cannon is a classic Mickey, formed by a hole and two bolts.

- Frontierland Shootin' Exposition

Hint 127: In front of the "Nancy's Dan" tombstone, three lobes of a cactus resemble a classic Mickey.

- Pioneer Mercantile shop

Hint 128: On the walls inside the gift shop, white river rocks at the lower center of some of the lamp covers (the ones with bears) form classic Mickeys.

Hint 129: At the left rear of the store, light brown gourds hang high on a pole at the left side of a cashier's counter. They are usually arranged to resemble a classic Mickey.

- Rancho del Zocalo Restaurante

Hint 130: Halfway up a wooden support post near the corner of a wall behind a condiment and napkin cart, you can spot a classic Mickey depression in the wood. You'll see it best by looking back in from the exit with the gate on the restaurant's right side (as you approach the restaurant from the main Frontierland walkway).

- River Belle Terrace restaurant

Hint 131: A classic Mickey cutout decorates the back of a child's highchair.

Main Street, U.S.A.

- *Plaza Inn restaurant*

Hint 132: To the right of the main entrance (as you enter), a framed painting of a floral arrangement includes an upside-down classic Mickey formed of roses.

- *Photo Supply Company*

Hint 133: On the middle of a high shelf behind the "Photo Preview" counter, a lens and two adjoining circles form a classic Mickey on the front of a camera.

- *Silhouette Studio*

Hint 134: In the front display window of the Silhouette Studio, the fancy frames on some of the displays include classic Mickeys. (These frames come and go, but a frame with classic Mickeys is usually on display.)

- *Fruit cart*

Hint 135: A green classic Mickey hides on an axle under a fruit cart that is usually positioned midway along Main Street near the Disney Clothiers shop.

- *Market House*

Hint 136: In the rear of the Market House, a side door leads to a Cast Member door. You'll find a light fixture with classic Mickeys on the wall just past the side door.

- *In and near Main Street Cinema*

Hint 137: Inside Main Street Cinema, some of the recessed lights on the sides of the step risers are shaped like classic Mickeys.

Hint 138: Outside, near Main Street Cinema, a "Casting Agency" sign on a door includes two classic Mickeys in the design, one at the top and one at the bottom.

- Main Street Magic Shop

Hint 139: Along the front counter inside the Magic Shop on the left, a white rope on a display shelf is coiled into a classic Mickey shape.

Hint 140: In an outside display window to the left of the Magic Shop's entrance, the ace on an Ace of Clubs playing card resembles a classic Mickey instead of a club.

- Penny Arcade

Hint 141: Inside in the rear section, a small classic Mickey hides between the play buttons on a game machine called "Pinocchio, Make Him Dance."

- Gibson Girl Ice Cream Parlor

Hint 142: A bejeweled lamp hangs from the ceiling at the rear of the parlor. Along the lower part of the lamp, jewels are positioned to form classic Mickeys.

- Blue Ribbon Bakery

Hint 143: In a painting on the rear wall behind the middle of the counter, look near a cow for a sack filled with fruit and vegetables. The large yellow fruit at the top of the sack forms a sideways classic Mickey with two limes.

- Emporium store

Hint 144: Classic Mickeys are at the top of ornate wire-framed bookstands in some of the store's outside display windows.

- Disneyland Railroad: Main Street Station

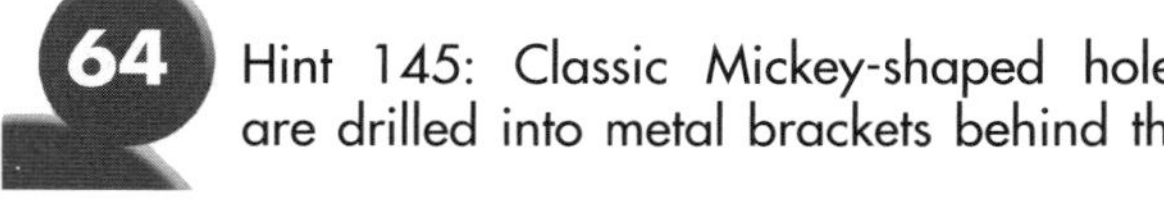

Hint 145: Classic Mickey-shaped holes are drilled into metal brackets behind the

conductor's cabin on top of several of the tender tanks, for example, "Fred Gurley's" Engine No. 3 and "Ward Kimball's" Engine No. 5. You can spot these classic Mickeys from the side waiting queue or from inside the first car.

Frontierland

- *Fantasmic!*

Hint 146: During the *Fantasmic!* show, a classic Mickey appears on the water screen, outlined by white foam. You can spot it just before the scene with Mickey and the whirlpool.

Fireworks show

Hint 147: Disneyland's fireworks show often features a cluster of three exploding shells that form a classic Mickey.

Entrance Plaza between the theme parks

Hint 148: Some of the engraved personalized brick plaques at your feet along the entrance plaza feature a bell design. The bell ringer is a classic Mickey. (You'll also find decorative Mickey images on these plaques.)

Hint 149: Take a look at the directional signpoles. You'll find classic Mickey indentations on the bottoms of some of them, while the tops of the poles sport Mickey ears.

CHAPTER 3

Disney California Adventure Scavenger Hunt

★ Arrive at the entrance turnstiles (with your admission ticket) 30 minutes before the official opening time.

★ Cross Sunshine Plaza and walk by "a bug's land" to Paradise Pier. Turn left and pass by Ariel's Grotto restaurant and then line up for ***Toy Story Midway Mania!***

Clue 1: Along the entrance queue, search for a tiny Hidden Mickey on a poster.
4 points

Clue 2: Spot a classic Mickey at the loading dock.
2 points

Clue 3: On the interactive screens, look behind the target balloons in front of the volcano for a classic Mickey.
5 points

Clue 4: Find Mickey after you exit your vehicle.
3 points

Clue 5: After you exit, search for Mickey ***on the promenade***.
4 points

★ Now walk to ***California Screamin'*** and ride if you're brave enough!

Clue 6: Stay alert while you're screaming for a classic Mickey below you on the ground.
4 points

Clue 7: Find Mickey on a sign along the exit.
2 points

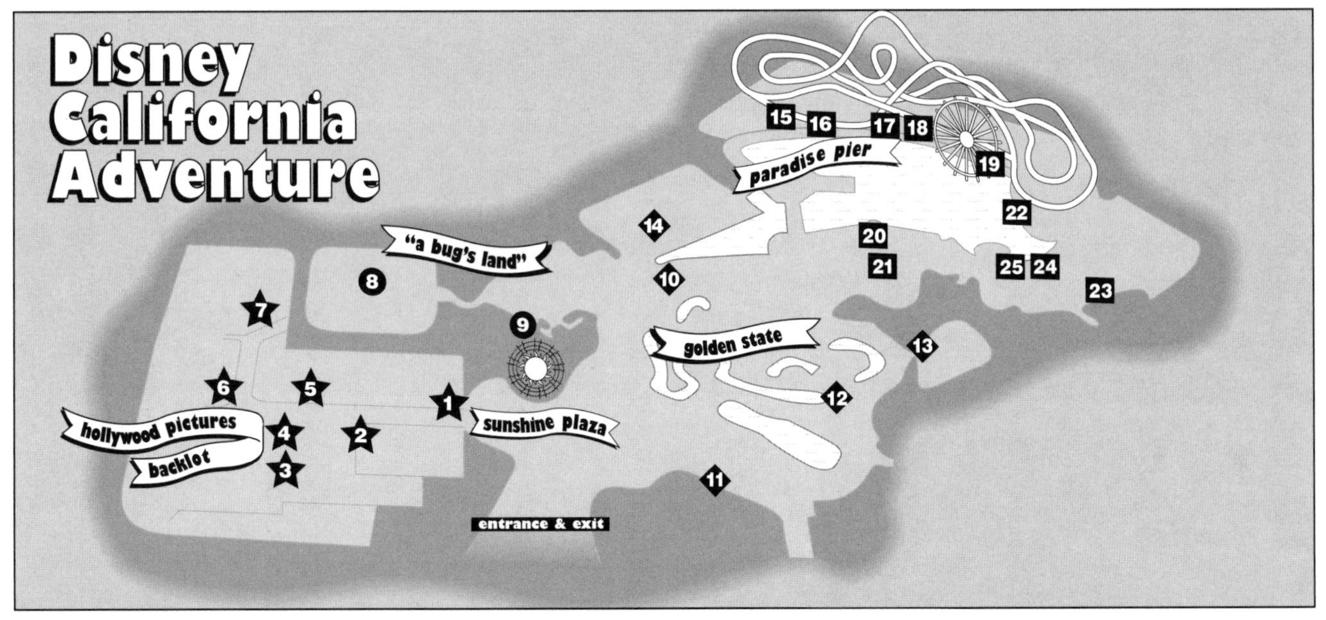
Disney California Adventure
"a bug's land"
paradise pier
golden state
sunshine plaza
hollywood pictures backlot
entrance & exit
1
2
3
4
5
6
7
8
9
10
11
12
13
14
15
16
17
18
19
20
21
22
23
24
25

sunshine plaza

★ hollywood pictures backlot

1 Disney Junior — Live on Stage!
2 MuppetVision 3D
3 Monsters, Inc. Mike & Sulley to the Rescue!
4 The Hollywood Backlot Stage
5 Disney Animation:
- Turtle Talk with Crush
- Animation Academy
- Character Close-Up
- Sorcerer's Workshop

6 Disney's Aladdin—A Musical Spectacular
7 The Twilight Zone Tower of Terror™

● "a bug's land"

8 Flik's Fun Fair:
- Tuck and Roll's Drive 'Em Buggies
- Francis' Ladybug Boogie
- Flik's Flyers
- Princess Dot Puddle Park
- Heimlich's Chew Chew Train

9 It's Tough to be a Bug!

◆ golden state

10 Walt Disney Imagineering Blue Sky Cellar
11 Soarin' Over California
12 Grizzly River Run
13 Redwood Creek Challenge Trail
14 The Bakery Tour

■ paradise pier

15 California Screamin'
16 King Triton's Carousel
17 Toy Story Midway Mania!
18 Games of the Boardwalk
19 Mickey's Fun Wheel
20 World of Color
21 The Little Mermaid — Ariel's Undersea Adventure
22 Silly Symphony Swings
23 Goofy's Sky School
24 Jumpin' Jellyfish
25 Golden Zephyr

★ Stroll past Ariel's Grotto restaurant to ***The Little Mermaid—Ariel's Undersea Adventure***.

Clue 8: Look for Mickey along the entrance queue.
2 points

Clue 9: Don't miss Mickey on the loading dock mural!
4 points

Clue 10: Check out the frogs along the ride!
4 points

★ Walk to the Golden State area and ride ***Soarin' Over California***. Or get a FASTPASS to ride later if the wait is more than 15 minutes.

Clue 11: Pay attention to the pre-show video for Mickey ears.
2 points

Clue 12: Also in the pre-show video, find some clothing characters.
4 points for two Hidden Characters

Clue 13: While on the ride, look left for a Mickey balloon.
4 points

Clue 14: Now quickly look right for a Mickey shadow on the golf course.
4 points

Clue 15: Watch the ball hurtling toward you.
5 points

Clue 16: Search the sky over the castle for a Hidden Mickey.
3 points

★ Walk back across Sunshine Plaza to Hollywood Pictures Backlot. Ride ***The Twilight Zone Tower of Terror™***.

Clues 17 and 18: Spot a Mickey doll during the pre-show and on the ride.
3 points for each sighting; 6 points total

Clue 19: In the boiler room before the elevator ride, look around for Mickey on a gauge.
3 points

Clue 20: Line up in front of the lower leftmost elevator and admire Mickey.
5 points

Clue 21: Find Mickey along the exit after the ride.
3 points

Clue 22: Say goodbye one last time to the little girl and her Mickey doll!
3 points

★ Go to ***Monsters, Inc. Mike & Sulley to the Rescue!*** and line up.

Clue 23: Study the inside queue walls for a Hidden Mickey.
3 points

Clue 24: Watch the pre-show video monitor in the queue for a Hidden Mickey.
3 points

Clue 25: Before you board your vehicle, spot those headlights again!
2 points

Clue 26: At the beginning of the ride, search the skyline for a tiny Hidden Mickey.
5 points

Clue 27: Don't miss the moving Mickey shadow on a wall along the ride!
5 points

Clue 28: Admire the color-changing Randall (the multi-legged lizard-shaped monster)!
5 bonus points

Clue 29: On the ride, look for a Hidden Mickey on Sulley.
4 points

Clue 30: Stay alert for Mickey near a monitor screen.
3 points

★ Stop by ***MuppetVision 3D***.

Clue 31: Watch for a Hidden Mickey in the pre-show.
3 points

Clue 32: Try to spot Mickey balloons during the show.
3 points

Clue 33: Study the license plate on the fire truck for a Hidden Surprise.
4 points

★ Walk to "a bug's land." Enjoy ***Heimlich's Chew Chew Train***.

Clue 34: Watch for Mickey in the rocks.
4 points

Clue 35: Search for Mickey on a snack stand in "a bug's land."
3 points

★ Consider lunch at the restaurant of your choice, or try one of the nearby counter-service eateries: Pacific Wharf Café (salads, chowders, etc.) or Cocina Cucamonga Mexican Grill.

★ While at lunch, check your Times Guide for the next show in Hyperion Theater (the show as we go to press is *Disney's Aladdin—A Musical Spectacular*) and a convenient show time for *Disney Junior—Live on Stage!*

★ At the time you've chosen, see the show at ***Hyperion Theater***.

Clue 36: Look around for a Hidden Mickey inside the theater, near the seats.
3 points

★ At a convenient time, visit ***Disney Junior—Live on Stage!***

Clue 37: Watch for Mickey images during the show.
3 points for two or more

★ Stroll to Paradise Pier and check out ***Jumpin' Jellyfish***.

Clue 38: Study the outside of the attraction for a classic Mickey.
4 points

★ Enter the ***Sideshow Shirts*** store, not far from *Mickey's Fun Wheel*.

Clue 39: Look around for a small Hidden Mickey near some nails.
4 points

Clue 40: Search for a Hidden Mickey on a wall inside the store.
4 points

★ Take a look inside the ***Man Hat n' Beach*** store.

Clue 41: Locate a Hidden Mickey on a merchandise stand.
3 points

★ Enter the ***Point Mugu Tattoo*** store.

Clue 42: Spot a Hidden Mickey on a wall.
3 points

★ Now stroll ***along the promenade***.

Clue 43: Search the *Games of the Boardwalk* buildings for a Hidden Mickey.
3 points

Clue 44: Find Donald Duck on the promenade outside *King Triton's Carousel*.
3 points

Clue 45: Locate a Mickey on a billboard.
2 points

★ Enter the ***Treasures in Paradise*** shop.

Clue 46: Find a Hidden Mickey on an animal inside the store.
2 points

Clue 47: Look for Mickey in a painting.
4 points

Clue 48: Stroll inside ***Ariel's Grotto*** restaurant and down the stairs to the right to locate Mickey.
3 points

Clue 49: Salute Mickey across from Ariel's Grotto.
2 points

★ Walk to ***The Bakery Tour*** nearby in Golden State.

Clue 50: Locate Mickey inside the entrance to the tour.
2 points

★ Check out ***Walt Disney Imagineering Blue Sky Cellar*** for some Hidden Mickeys.

Clue 51: Study the sign outside.
4 points

Clue 52: Now admire Mickey in the first mural inside.
4 points

Clue 53: Find a classic Mickey in the main room.
3 points

Clue 54: Then look for Mickey on Tow Mater ***across from Blue Sky Cellar***.
4 points

★ Mosey straight ahead (toward Paradise Pier) to the ***Redwood Creek Challenge Trail***.

Clue 55: Tarry at the large trail map just inside the entrance and spot three classic Mickeys.
5 points for finding all three

Clue 56: Mickey is near a cave inside the trail area.
3 points

★ Check out the ***Rushin' River Outfitters*** shop near *Grizzly River Run*.

Clue 57: Search for Hidden Mickeys on the merchandise inside the shop.
3 points

★ Walk past the entrance to *Grizzly River Run* to the ***fence overlooking the raft stream***.

Clue 58: Investigate the area near the fence for a Hidden Mickey.
4 points

★ Amble over to the ***Taste Pilots' Grill***.

Clue 59: Study the walls inside to find two Hidden Mickeys.
2 points each; 4 points total

★ Cross Sunshine Plaza to Hollywood Pictures Backlot, and then stand outside the ***Disney Animation Building***.

Clue 60: Look up for a Hidden Mickey on a pole.
3 points

Clue 61: Now search for Mickey on the outside wall of the Animation Building.
2 points total for one or more

Clue 62: Spot Hidden Mickeys along the Animation Building's entrance hall.
3 points total for one or more

Clue 63: Search for a classic Hidden Mickey inside the ***Animation Academy***.
3 points

Clue 64: Walk through the ***Sorcerer's Workshop*** to locate two Hidden Mickeys on the wall.
4 points for finding both

Clue 65: Find two Hidden Mickeys in the wall posters outside.
4 points for spotting both

Clue 66: Study the pictures in the glass nearby for a classic Mickey.
3 points

Clue 67: Search a display window nearby for a Hidden Mickey.
3 points

Clue 68: Look for Mickey on the ceiling inside ***Off the Page***.
4 points

★ Cross the street to ***Schmoozies***.

Clues 69 and 70: Check out the outside walls for Hidden Mickeys.
5 points total for finding two Hidden Mickeys

Clue 71: Walk to the ***Studio Store*** near the entrance to *MuppetVision 3D* and find a Hidden Mickey.
4 points

★ Return to ***Sunshine Plaza*** to find more Hidden Mickeys.

Clue 72: Carefully study the pavement in front of the ***Sun Fountain*** for a Hidden Mickey.
5 points

Clue 73: Search for another Hidden Mickey under a cement bench.
5 points

Clue 74: Find some Hidden Mickeys near trees.
2 points total

★ Enter the ***Greetings from California*** store.

Clue 75: Spot Mickey on a reel of film.
2 points

Clue 76: In the next room, spot Mickey on a car.
4 points

Clue 77: Find a camera Hidden Mickey in the following room.
3 points

Clues 78 and 79: Look around inside the next room for two underwater Mickeys.
4 points for spotting both

Clue 80: In this same room, glance up for Mickey.
3 points

Clue 81: Search for Tinker Bell on a wall.
4 points

Clue 82: In the next room, locate two Mickeys on the beach.
4 points for spotting both

Clue 83: Outside Greetings from California, search high for a Hidden Mickey.
4 points

Clue 84: Walk over to the ***Engine-Ears Toys*** store and locate Mickey on an outside sign.
2 points

Clue 85: Inside the store, find two classic Mickeys on the walls.
5 points for spotting both

Clue 86: Spot a Hidden Mickey on the wall inside ***Baker's Field Bakery***.
2 points

★ Exit Disney California Adventure Park to the ***main entrance plaza***.

Clue 87: Look over the trees in the entrance plaza for Hidden Mickeys.
3 points

Clue 88: Check out some ticket buildings for Hidden Mickeys.
2 points

★ Rest, relax, have some dinner and plan on returning for the ***World of Color*** show in Paradise Bay.

Clue 89: Watch the nightly *World of Color* show in Paradise Bay to spot a Mickey balloon.
5 points

Total Points for Disney California Adventure Park =

How'd You Do?

Up to 118 points – Bronze
119 to 234 points – Silver
235 points and over – Gold
294 points – Perfect Score

You may have done even better if you earned bonus points in *Monsters, Inc. Mike & Sulley to the Rescue.*

Paradise Pier

- *Toy Story Midway Mania!*

Hint 1: Along the inside part of the winding entrance queue, spots near a blue dinosaur's left eye and upper horn form a classic Mickey, tilted to the right. The dino, Trixie from *Toy Story*, is near the right lower corner of a poster labeled "Dino Darts."

Hint 2: On the wall at the loading area, a classic Mickey is formed by three picture frames with *Toy Story* characters.

Hint 3: Watch for the screen with target balloons in front of the volcano spewing lava. If you pop the middle 100-point balloon on the second tier, a light classic Mickey appears on the rear surface in the lava behind the balloons.

Hint 4: Along the exit walkway from the ride, a "Toy Story Midway" game sits on a rug in a display room to the left. On the left side of the game box, three ovals (containing pictures of Jessie, Rex, and Bullseye the horse) form a classic Mickey.

- *On the promenade*

Hint 5: Across from *Toy Story Midway Mania!*, Steamboat Willie Mickey is pictured on faux newspapers stacked at a drink stand.

- *California Screamin'*

Hint 6: When you're upside down in the loop, look at the ground to your left for a classic Mickey cement footing at the base of one of the vertical support poles. You can also spot this Mickey if you look right as you ride through the little hills that cover the *Toy Story Midway Mania!* attraction building.

Hint 7: Classic Mickeys are atop the frames of the sample photos on the sign advertising the California ScreamCam. (Note: You can see this Hidden Mickey without riding the coaster.)

- *The Little Mermaid— Ariel's Undersea Adventure*

Hint 8: Classic Mickey circles hide in the design of the ironwork along the sides of the upper support for the entrance queue cover.

Hint 9: A small classic Mickey is impressed in a large rock at the lower left corner of the loading dock mural, just above the green tile. You can spot this Hidden Mickey from the entrance queue and again as you pass by it on your right in your seashell vehicle.

Hint 10: Toward the end of the ride, check the pond (to your right) for frogs with dark spots on their backs that form sideways classic Mickeys.

Golden State

- *Soarin' Over California*

Hint 11: In the pre-show video, a man is asked to remove his Mickey Mouse ears.

Hint 12: Also in the pre-show, a boy sitting in his ride seat is wearing a shirt with a Grumpy logo and shorts sporting Mickey Mouse.

Hint 13: When you soar over the hills and spot a golf course, look immediately to your lower left and find a golf cart. The man standing on the other side of the cart is holding a blue Mickey balloon.

Hint 14: Look to the right side of the golf course. About halfway along the fairway is a slightly distorted shadow classic Mickey on the green grass formed by a cluster of three trees. The "ears" of the shadow Mickey touch the right side of the white cart path.

Hint 15: Look straight ahead and down to the golf course. Spot the man about to swing a golf club. When he strikes the golf ball, it will head directly toward you. Watch the ball's rotation to see the dark classic Mickey on the surface of the ball.

Hint 16: You complete your *Soarin'* ride over Disneyland. Watch the evening fireworks explode before you; the second burst forms a huge classic Mickey in the sky.

Hollywood Pictures Backlot

- *The Twilight Zone Tower of Terror™*

Hint 17: In the pre-show video in the library, the little girl is holding a Mickey doll.

Hint 18: On the ride, the little girl appears again, still holding the Mickey doll in her right hand.

Hint 19: After you leave the library pre-show video room and soon after you enter the basement boiler room, check the right side of the aisle for a group of circular gauges. One gauge in the group has a black classic Mickey shape at the end of a needle pointing to the right. It's easier to see from the lower level queue.

Hint 20: Above the lower loading area for the leftmost elevator, a classic Mickey made of three spotlights is projected on the ceiling grate.

Hint 21: Circles on the front of some of the cameras in displays along the exit form classic Mickeys. One acceptable image is on a camera in the leftmost display window under the ride photo review monitors. Another is behind the photo purchase counter on a camera on the second shelf to the right of the recessed area.

Hint 22: As you leave the gift shop, you can wave goodbye to the girl and her Mickey doll from the Tower of Terror story. The two are at the exit in a photo on the wall to the left of the photo purchase counter.

- Monsters, Inc. Mike & Sulley to the Rescue!

Hint 23: On the "Monstropolis Cab Co." wall poster, the taxicab headlights form an upside-down classic Mickey.

Hint 24: During the video loop on the queue monitors, a taxi appears with the words "Please Proceed" on the front bumper. The headlights of this vehicle are shaped like upside-down classic Mickeys.

Hint 25: The taxi with the upside-down headlight classic Mickeys is pictured on the side of your vehicle.

Hint 26: As your vehicle begins to move, look at the skyline behind a tall wall to your left. A tiny black classic Mickey is visible through holes along the top of the wall. Look along the skyline. You'll find this Mickey below the green "Downtown" sign and to the left of a tall vertical pipe behind the wall.

Hint 27: To the left of your ride vehicle, a side-profile shadow of the main mouse moves from left to right along the windows in the wall of the Harryhausen's restaurant scene.

Hint 28: Watch for "Boo" on top of Randall's back. She pounds on Randall's head with a bat, causing his camouflage coloration to change continually. At one point, his body turns lime green (or sometimes yellow) with a blue (or purple) classic Mickey spot on his belly above a lower leg. (Note: This great image is visible only intermittently and not on every ride-through. Good luck!).

Hint 29: Sulley appears several times during the ride. A dark classic Mickey marking is on Sulley's left upper thigh the last time he appears (by the pink door).

Hint 30: Near the end of the ride, a classic Mickey is formed by dials and gauges on a control panel under the right monitor screen.

- *MuppetVision 3D*

Hint 31: Early in the pre-show on the monitors, check the screen for a test pattern with a classic Mickey shape.

Hint 32: Near the end of the movie, after the cannon shoots holes in the theater, some of the observers outside are holding Mickey balloons.

Hint 33: Near the end of the movie, an image of Sleeping Beauty Castle (a Hidden Surprise) is on a license plate at the right lower corner of the fire truck Kermit is riding.

"a bug's land"

- *Heimlich's Chew Chew Train*

Hint 34: Near the end of the ride, the train stops prior to re-entering the station. Three rocks in the shape of a classic Mickey are embedded in a hill to the right of the ride vehicle. If you are seated in row 4, the Hidden Mickey will be close by.

Hint 35: A classic Mickey made of cherries is on the front of a fruit drink stand, which is often located near *Heimlich's Chew Chew Train*.

Hollywood Pictures Backlot

- *Hyperion Theater*

Hint 36: Classic Mickeys are at the top center of frames over several of the doors inside the theater.

- *Disney Junior—Live on Stage!*

Hint 37: Classic Mickeys appear at times in the lighting and stage effects and on various stage props during the live show.

Paradise Pier

- *Jumpin' Jellyfish*

Hint 38: Bubbles on a support pole on the right (as you face the attraction) form a sideways classic Mickey. You can see it best from the right side of the attraction.

- *Sideshow Shirts store*

Hint 39: Toward the front of the store, find a painting of a man lying on a bed of nails. A small classic Mickey is in the wood on the side of the bed.

Hint 40: A painting of a woman named Betty is on the rear wall of the store. A classic Mickey is etched in the wood on the middle of the right side of the picture frame.

- *Man Hat n' Beach store*

Hint 41: On a merchandise stand inside the store, a classic Mickey is on the back of an octopus's head.

- Point Mugu Tattoo store

Hint 42: On the rear wall near the ceiling, a classic Mickey hides on a sign between the words "Paradise" and "Pier."

- Along the promenade

Hint 43: White classic Mickey designs are under the high eaves of the *Games of the Boardwalk* building with the "Paradise Pier Amusements Co." sign.

Hint 44: A row of Donald Ducks is atop each of two large gazebo shelters next to the lake near *King Triton's Carousel.*

Hint 45: A classic Mickey on a roller coaster support is on the left side of the billboard close to the ice cream shop and not far from Ariel's Grotto restaurant.

- Treasures in Paradise shop

Hint 46: A classic Mickey adorns the side and bottom on a lion's saddle in a store display.

Hint 47: In the "Azalea" painting of a lady behind a service counter, a classic Mickey is formed by circles in the area where the wide belt loops connect below her waist.

- Ariel's Grotto restaurant

Hint 48: Along the wall across from the bottom of the staircase inside the restaurant, white classic Mickey bubbles hide at the lower left of the display sign for "Ariel's Grotto Disney Princess Celebration."

-Across from Ariel's Grotto

Hint 49: At the rear of Duffy the Disney Bear's greeting gazebo is a classic Mickey on a wall. He's made of a porthole and two round lights. Other Mickey images also decorate the gazebo, both inside and out.

Golden State

- *The Bakery Tour*

Hint 50: On a table in a corner of the first room, you'll see bread rolls. Sometimes they're shaped like Mickey; other times they're imprinted with him.

- *Walt Disney Imagineering Blue Sky Cellar*

Hint 51: On a sign outside, a tiny classic Mickey hides at the lower left in the swirling path of sparkles.

Hint 52: A cloud image of Sorcerer Mickey is at the lower left of the blue mural just inside the entrance.

Hint 53: A black classic Mickey lies on a paint palette in an Imagineering art display in the main room.

- *Across from Blue Sky Cellar*

Hint 54: In Tow Mater's Character Greeting area, a classic Mickey wing nut is on top of the air cleaner on his engine.

- *Redwood Creek Challenge Trail*

Hint 55: You'll find three classic Mickeys on the left side of the trail map. A group of three rocks in a stream forms a Hidden Mickey at the top left of the map. Three circles in the middle left form a classic Mickey in foam (look just to left of the mouth of the left water slide). Lower down, three log seats in the Ahwahnee Camp Circle are arranged to create a classic Mickey.

Hint 56: At the rear of the trail area, three gray rocks embedded in the ground in front of Kenai's Spirit Cave form a classic Mickey.

- *Rushin' River Outfitters shop*

Hint 57: On some of the stuffed grizzly bears, the rear pads on the bottoms of the

paws are shaped like classic Mickeys.

- *Near Grizzly River Run entrance*

Hint 58: A classic Mickey made of rocks is embedded in the pavement under the right side of the fence, close to the "Grizzly Peak Recreation Area" cabin.

- *Taste Pilots' Grill*

Hint 59: A photo of an engine shows a classic Mickey shape. The photo is in two places: to the left of the food order area over an exit door and also to the right of the food order area on the right rear wall.

Hollywood Pictures Backlot

- *Disney Animation Building*

Hint 60: A small classic Mickey sits atop the flagpole over the front of the Animation Building.

Hint 61: Along the top of some outside windows and wall pillars, classic Mickey "hats" are in the tile design.

Hint 62: In the mosaic lettering on the entrance (and exit) walls, large and small circles form many classic Mickeys.

Hint 63: A drum set shaped like a classic Mickey sits on a shelf high above the stage inside the *Animation Academy.* You'll also find many decorative Mickey images on and around the stage.

Hint 64: In the *Sorcerer's Workshop* area, Sorcerer Mickey is on the left wall toward the end of the room. He's encircled by classic Mickey bubbles. Nearby on the left wall, you'll find a classic Mickey intertwined with the middle of a treble clef.

Hint 65: Shadows of boys with Mickey ears decorate the bottoms of two posters on the wall outside; one poster is entitled

"Turtle Talk" and the other "Toy Story Zoetrope."

Hint 66: In the tall green glass wall outside, an upside-down classic Mickey made of specks of pixie dust floats above and to the left of the rightmost fairy godmother's pointed hat. The Hidden Mickey is about halfway up the right side of the glass wall.

- *Off the Page shop*

Hint 67: In an outside display window of the shop, the last of several Dalmatians has an upside-down classic Mickey made of spots on its rear thigh.

Hint 68: On a drawing hanging from the ceiling in the middle of Off the Page, bubbles form a classic Mickey in front of the shadow of an alligator's front leg.

- *Schmoozies*

Hint 69: Face Schmoozies from the street, and then walk to the left side of the snack shop. There are two murals on the left wall. The one on the right has classic Mickeys formed by round pieces of colored glass.

Hint 70: Now face the shop from Hollywood Boulevard. A classic Mickey formed by three tan stones hides to the right of a knife tip and above a pink cup on the right side of the rightmost mural on the front of the shop. This Mickey is above a pink cup.

- *Studio Store*

Hint 71: A classic Mickey formed of photo frames hides on an inside wall. You'll find it above and to the left of a window that faces the main boulevard.

Sunshine Plaza

- *Sun Fountain*

Hint 72: As you stand facing the Sun Fountain, look at the straight "rays" in the cement that have glass pieces embedded in them. Find the second ray from the right side. A small, light brown classic Mickey lies in the cement about 10 to 12 feet from the fountain and several inches to the left of this second ray.

Hint 73: Face away from the Sun Fountain and locate a cement bench to your right that surrounds a planted area. A small classic Mickey is etched in the ground under the right side of the round lip that juts out from the bench.

Hint 74: Grates around the bases of trees in Sunshine Plaza and elsewhere have classic Mickey circles.

- *Greetings from California store*

Hint 75: In the room next to the candy store, a classic Mickey lies at the center of a large film reel that hangs from the ceiling above a checkout area.

Hint 76: In the "K-GOOF" wall mural, a black classic Mickey hides on the rear bumper of Goofy's car.

Hint 77: In one of the store's middle rooms, a huge camera on a wall has a small, black classic Mickey on its flashbulb.

Hint 78: Go to the store's photo preview and pickup area and check out the Goofy mural on the left wall, left of the counters. A classic Mickey floats in a bubble above Goofy's head.

Hint 79: On the opposite side of the room, another mural includes a black classic Mickey snorkeling on Mickey's swim trunks.

Hint 80: Stand at the photo pickup desk with the Goofy underwater mural to your left. A purple classic Mickey is on the ceiling above you amid the recessed lights.

Hint 81: On the right side of the wall behind the "PhotoPass Preview & Order" area, a tiny Tinker Bell flies above a wave near the right corner of the wall.

Hint 82: Classic Mickeys lie in the sand in the lower right of two beach murals. The murals are on opposite sides of the room.

Hint 83: Outside the store, to the left of the first "Greetings from California" sign, look for a sign that says "Premiere" and pictures a stylized theater with searchlights and a ticket booth. A small white classic Mickey is the ticket seller in the booth. He's in the middle window, under the word "Premiere."

- *Engine-Ears Toys*

Hint 84: On the sign above the store entrance doors, a Mickey hat is formed by a blue dome (behind the words "Engine-Ears Toys") and two train-wheel "ears" above it.

Hint 85: In the middle of the store and to the left, a classic Mickey shadow is under a large orange on a framed "Paradise Pier" poster. Nearby on a round "Golden State" poster, a tiny classic Mickey made of water droplets is at the upper right of a grapefruit half.

- *Baker's Field Bakery*

Hint 86: In a display on the wall to the right, a plate and two dishes form a classic Mickey.

Hint 87: Ironwork gratings surround some tree trunks in the entrance plaza. Tiny classic Mickey fasteners hold the ironwork bands in place.

Hint 88: In the general entrance plaza, you'll find classic Mickey holes inside the braces that support the ticket-booth counters.

Paradise Bay

- *World of Color show*

Hint 89: Watch for the *Up* scene on the water screen during the *World of Color* show. After the *Up* house has floated off the screen, a Mickey balloon soars up and sails off in the direction of the house.

CHAPTER 4

Downtown Disney District & Resort Hotel Scavenger Hunt

Because you may want to hunt only one area at a time, I've listed the perfect score for each area in parentheses after its name in the Clues section.

Downtown Disney District (40 points)

Begin your Downtown Disney search at about 11:00 a.m. to give yourself time to complete this hunt.

★Enter the ***D Street*** store.

Clue 1: Look around for Mickey on a wall.
3 points

★ Check out the ***Disney Vault 28*** shop.

Clue 2: Locate a classic Mickey in a window of the store.
3 points

Clue 3: Search for two Mickeys on a wall.
5 points for finding both

★ Your next stop is ***Marceline's Confectionery***.

Clue 4: Find a Hidden Mickey outside the store.
3 points

★ Stop into ***Studio Disney 365*** store.

Clue 5: Search for four Hidden Mickeys on a mirror.
5 points for finding all four

★ Continue on to ***Naples Ristorante e Pizzeria***.

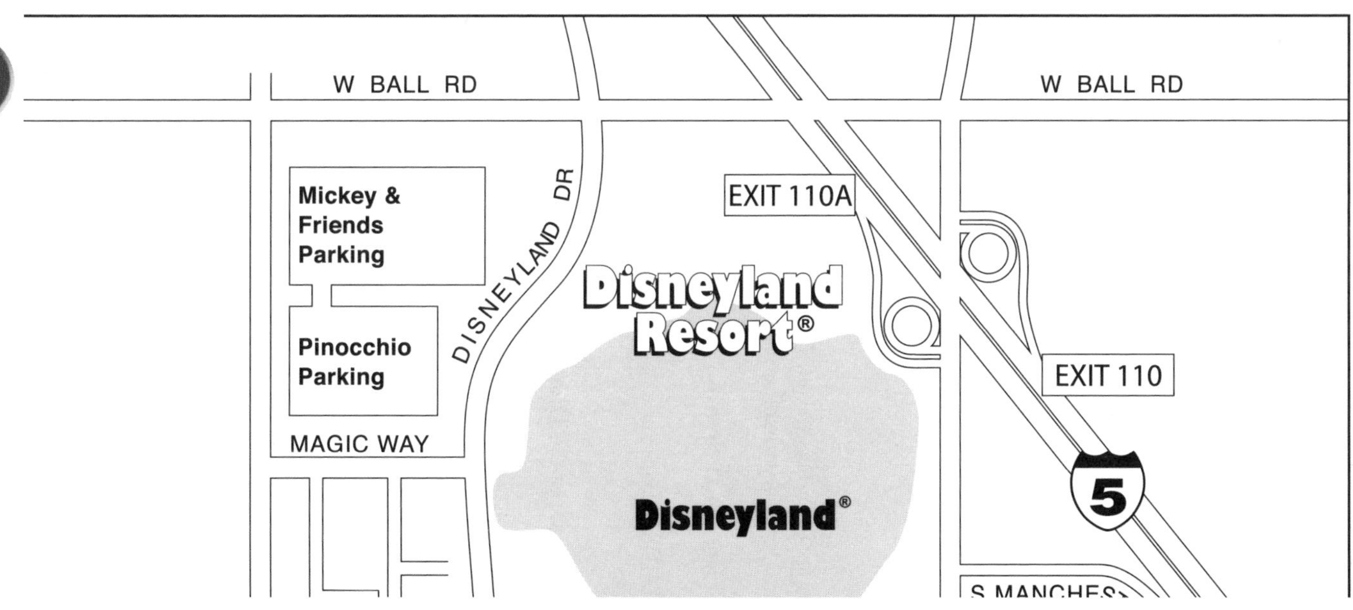
W BALL RD
W BALL RD
Mickey & Friends Parking
Pinocchio Parking
MAGIC WAY
DISNEYLAND DR
EXIT 110A
Disneyland Resort®
Disneyland®
EXIT 110
5

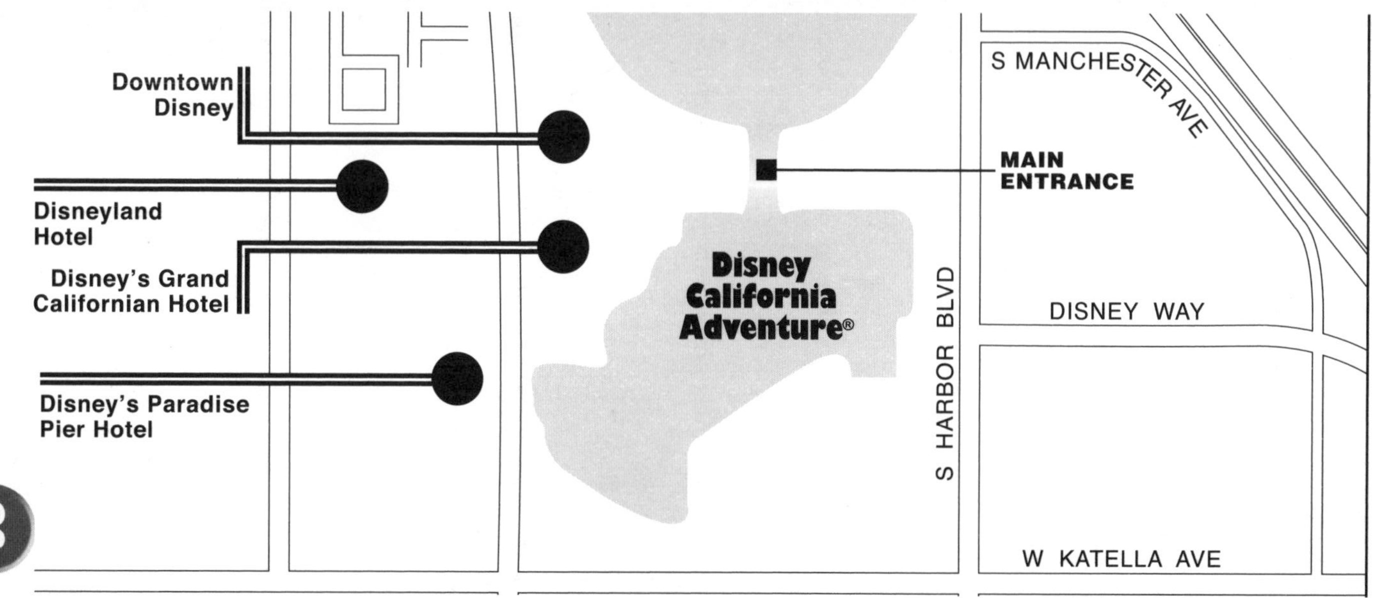
Downtown Disney
Disneyland Hotel
Disney's Grand Californian Hotel
Disney's Paradise Pier Hotel
Disney California Adventure®
MAIN ENTRANCE
S HARBOR BLVD
S MANCHESTER AVE
DISNEY WAY
W KATELLA AVE

Clue 6: Look up for Mickey outside the restaurant.
3 points

★ Walk to the ***Quiksilver*** store.

Clue 7: Search for a Hidden Mickey outside the store.
4 points

★ Stroll over to the ***World of Disney*** store nearby.

Clue 8: Find Hidden Mickeys outside the store.
1 point

Clue 9: Locate a classic Mickey near the ceiling in the Princess room in the middle of the store.
4 points

Clue 10: Now look for Mickeys on another mural in the Princess room.
5 points for finding seven

Clue 11: Find Mickey on some merchandise stands.
2 points

Clue 12: Study the kiosks near the entrance plaza.
2 points

★ Now head for the ***Mickey & Friends Parking Structure*** to find more Hidden Mickeys. You can walk there or take a tram from Downtown Disney.

Mickey & Friends Parking Structure (21 points)

Clue 13: Stop and look up at the directional sign on the walkway near the tram stop.
2 points

Clue 14: Inside the parking structure, walk up to Level 2 (Daisy Level) and find a Hidden Mickey between poles 3A and 3B.
5 points

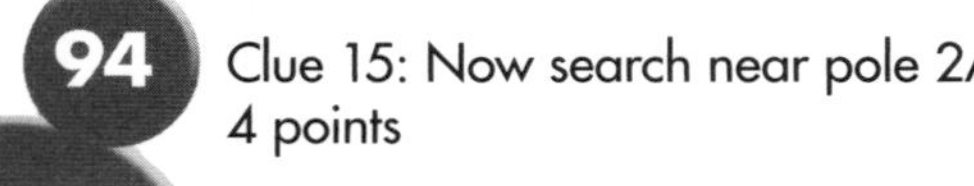

Clue 15: Now search near pole 2A.
4 points

Clue 16: Look around for Mickey on a sign.
3 points

Clue 17: The address for Disneyland and Mickey & Friends Parking Structure is 1313 S. Harbor Blvd. Since 'M' is the thirteenth letter, two 13's correspond to two 'M's, Mickey Mouse's initials.
5 points if you can find the address posted

★ Hop on the ***tram to the parks***.

Clue 18: Spot Mickey on a pole.
2 points

★ Make your way back to Downtown Disney, then walk over to ***Disney's Grand Californian Hotel*** & Spa.

Disney's Grand Californian Hotel & Spa
(74 points)

Clue 19: Outside the main entrance, look for Mickey's face on a panel.
5 points

Clue 20: In this same area, find a classic Mickey on a panel.
3 points

★ Now ***enter the lobby***.

Clue 21: Search low for a Hidden Mickey.
3 points

Clue 22: Study the front of the main registration counters for a "conductor Mickey."
5 points

Clue 23: Now search the front of these registration counters for a classic Mickey.
4 points

Clue 24: Search the front of the registration counters for a Hidden Tinker Bell.
5 points

Clue 25: Glance behind the main registration counters for a classic Mickey on a tree.
4 points

Clue 26: Look for two other classic Mickeys behind the main registration counters.
4 points for finding both

Clue 27: Search the other registration counter at the far left (as you face the main registration counter) for two Hidden Mickeys.
4 points for finding both

Clue 28: Find a Hidden Mickey facing the main lobby.
5 points

Clue 29: Spot a Mickey image on a desk.
3 points

Clue 30: Locate Hidden Mickeys on telephones.
2 points for spotting two or more

Clue 31: Find Mickey on a map.
3 points

Clue 32: Look for Mickey in the hallway with the restrooms not far from the registration counters.
4 points

Clue 33: Search for Mickey near the fireplace.
3 points

Clue 34: Find four Mickey images on a ship.
4 points for finding all four

★ Enter the ***Hearthstone Lounge***.

Clue 35: Check around for a Hidden Mickey.
2 points

★ If you're hungry, snack inside Hearthstone Lounge or try to get seated for lunch at Storytellers Café.

★ Stroll through the ***Downtown Disney exit doors*** and turn around.

Clue 36: Look up for a Hidden Mickey.
4 points

Clue 37: Now locate Mickey close to the walkway.
2 points

★ Return to the main lobby and take the ***exit that leads to Disney California Adventure*** Park.

Clue 38: After a few steps, look up for Mickey.
3 points

★ Now head back to the Grand Californian once more and stroll out the front entrance to ***Disneyland Drive*** (which will take you over to Disney's Paradise Pier Hotel if you are up for more Mickey hunting now).

Clue 39: Find Mickey on a sign.
2 points

★ Stroll over to ***Disney's Paradise Pier Hotel***.

Disney's Paradise Pier Hotel
(45 points)

Clue 40: Spot Mickey on a wall outside the front entrance of the hotel.
4 points

★ Step ***inside the hotel***.

Clue 41: Spot Mickey in the main lobby.
4 points

Clue 42: Look for a wall painting inside the hotel with a Hidden Mickey.
3 points

Clue 43: Spot Mickey near the fitness center and the Beachcomber Club.
4 points for both

Clue 44: Find a Hidden Mickey near the elevators.
3 points

Clue 45: Mickey is near the swimming pool.
2 points

Clue 46: Don't miss Mickey in the Game Room!
2 points

Clue 47: Locate Mickey in a photo in a hallway near the lobby.
5 points

★ Search for classic Mickeys in ***Disney's PCH Grill*** restaurant.

Clue 48: Study the carpet.
2 points

Clue 49: Search for Mickeys of different sizes in the wall décor.
3 points for finding both sizes

Clue 50: Look for Mickey on lamps.
2 points

Clue 51: Find Mickey in a picture.
1 point

Clue 52: Spot two Mickeys on the ceiling.
2 points for spotting both

Clue 53: Search for three camouflaged Mickeys on three separate surfboards.
5 points for sleuthing out all three

Clue 54: Find two Mickeys on entrance doors.
2 points for spotting both

★ Search ***outside the hotel's rear entrance***.

Clue 55: You can't miss Mickey outside the first-floor rear entrance.
1 point

★ Your final stop is the ***Disneyland Hotel***.

Disneyland Hotel
(69 points)

★ Check out the ***lobby and entrance areas***.

Clue 56: Inside the main hotel lobby, look down for three Hidden Mickeys.
2 points for each one; 6 points total

Clue 57: Study the lobby walls for Hidden Mickeys.
4 points

★ Step ***outside the front entrance***.

Clue 58: Spot Hidden Mickeys in the nearby parking lot.
1 point

Clue 59: While you're at the hotel entrance, don't miss Mickey on the luggage carts.
1 point

★ Take the ***central lobby elevator*** down a floor and look around.

Clue 60: Can you spot two Hidden Mickeys, one complete and one partial?
4 points for finding both

★ Find Mickey inside the ***main lobby gift shops***.

Clue 61: Peer around for side-profile Mickeys.
3 points for one or more

Clue 62: Say hello to Mickey and friends at the entrance to Donald's Gifts and Sundries.
3 points for spotting four characters

Clue 63: Study nearby telephones for Hidden Mickeys.
2 points

★ Search for Mickey in the ***Guest Services office*** near the main lobby.

Clue 64: Find Mickey images in five different locations in the office.
5 points for spotting all five

★ Now look ***around the hotel complex*** to find more Hidden Mickeys.

Clue 65: Locate Mickey in the pay telephone area.
1 point

Clue 66: Spot two Hidden Mickeys in the Convention Center area.
2 points for finding both

Clue 67: Peer inside Goofy's Theater for Hidden Mickeys.
3 points for finding three different sizes

Clue 68: Search the floor near Goofy's Kitchen for a Hidden Mickey.
5 points

Clue 69: Don't overlook Mickey on the stair handrail!
1 point

Clue 70: Look up for two Mickey images at the top of a staircase.
4 points for both

Clue 71: Near the Magic Kingdom Ballroom upstairs from Goofy's Kitchen, find a painting of Toontown on the wall and study it to spot two Hidden Mickeys.
4 points for finding both

Clue 72: In a painting nearby of a *Splash Mountain* scene, look for three Hidden Mickeys.
5 points for spotting all three

Clue 73: Stroll the hotel hallways ***near the Sleeping Beauty Pavilion*** for Hidden Mickeys at your feet.
2 points

Clue 74: Look around for two more Mickey images near telephones close to the Sleeping Beauty Pavilion.
4 points for finding both

Clue 75: Near the Sleeping Beauty Pavilion, scrutinize a painting of a jungle temple for a Hidden Mickey.
5 points

Clue 76: Explore the lobby areas of the hotel's other two towers for two more Hidden Mickeys.
4 points for both

Total Points for Downtown Disney and the Resort Hotels =

How'd You Do?

A perfect score for this scavenger hunt is 249. But here is a breakdown by area, so that you can compare your score with the perfect score for the areas you've covered. You'll find the perfect score for each section in parentheses. Give yourself gold if you score at least 80% of the total available points. (That would be 199 if you covered all five areas.)

Downtown Disney (40)
Mickey & Friends Parking Structure (21)
Disney's Grand Californian Hotel & Spa (74)
Disney's Paradise Pier Hotel (45)
Disneyland Hotel (69)

Notes

**Caution:
Don't peek at this section unless you really want help!**

Downtown Disney District

- D Street

Hint 1: A large classic Mickey shaped of faux bricks is located on a recessed wall behind a store register. This Hidden Mickey is often partially covered by paintings.

- Disney Vault 28

Hint 2: A classic Mickey head hides above crossbones in the window just below the right side of the large "Disney Vault 28" outdoor sign.

Hint: 3 A tiny classic Mickey is stuck on the upper right of the large metal vault door that forms the back wall of the entrance vestibule of the store, while an upside-down classic Mickey can be found on the vault door's lower right.

- *Marceline's Confectionery*

Hint 4: On the sign in front of the store, swirls in the letters "M" and "C" combine to form a classic Mickey.

- *Studio Disney 365*

Hint 5: As you enter the store, you'll find a framed mirror inside in a small dressing room to the left. Check the frame for classic Mickeys formed by embedded gems. One tilted left is in the top middle of the frame (red head, white ears), another tilted left is in the middle right side (red head, white ears). There's a third at the middle bottom (blue head, white ears) and a fourth (upside down) at the bottom right (white head, maroon ears).

- *Naples Ristorante e Pizzeria*

Hint 6: In front of the restaurant, near the top edge of the pizza sign at the "1:00 o'clock" position, three circular pepperonis form a sideways classic Mickey.

- *Quiksilver store*

Hint: 7 Outside in front of the store, a classic Mickey in the cement walkway is directly below a vertical red surfboard on the wall.

- *World of Disney*

Hint 8: Blue classic Mickeys adorn the corners of the large sign over the entrance doorway to the store.

Hint 9: In a mural near the ceiling on the left side of the Princess room, a white classic Mickey hides on an archway to the right of several Dalmatians.

Hint 10: Seven small red classic Mickeys are on a mural of the world behind the service counter in the Princess room.

Hint: 11 As in many shops on Disney property, classic Mickey holes are in some of the merchandise pole supports.

- Kiosks near the entrance plaza

Hint 12: The eaves of several kiosks sport classic Mickey-shaped supports.

Mickey & Friends Parking Structure

Hint 13: On the walkway near the tram stop, a classic Mickey sits atop the sign that points the way to Mickey & Friends Parking Structure.

Hint 14: A classic Mickey is etched in the cement between poles 3A and 3B, next to an unnumbered pole and under an "Emergency" sign.

Hint 15: A classic Mickey is etched in the cement two car stalls over from pole 2A, as you head toward the exit drive path.

Hint 16: Inside on the parking structure walls, a black classic Mickey is atop the yellow "Caution U-Turn" signs.

Hint 17: Ask a Cast Member where you can find the posted address—"1313"—on Mickey & Friends Parking Structure.

- Tram to the parks

Hint 18: Classic Mickeys top the light poles that line the tram path from the Mickey & Friends Parking Structure to the parks.

Disney's Grand Californian Hotel & Spa

- Outside the main entrance

Hint 19: A pillar just outside the main entrance is covered with colorful panels. On the rear panel, a three-quarter image of Mickey's face looks out from between the outer branches of a tree. He's about three-quarters of the way up the left side of the tree.

Hint 20: On this same rear panel, a classic Mickey is at the middle bottom of the tree, just above the trunk.

- Lobby area and nearby hallways

Hint 21: As you enter the Grand Californian lobby, look for a rug with the hotel's tree logo to spot the small classic Mickey above the tree's trunk.

Hint 22: A small side view of Mickey Mouse is sculpted in tile on the front desk. Toward the middle of the long counter, look for dancing bears on a panel in a depression in the desk. Mickey Mouse is conducting with a wand to the right of the white bear.

Hint 23: To the right of "conductor Mickey" is a brown, raised classic Mickey on the lower middle part of a tree.

Hint 24: To the left of "conductor Mickey" is a figure of Tinker Bell near (and to the immediate left of) a flat, dark writing surface.

Hint 25: On a fabric mural on the far left side of the rear wall behind the main registration counters, a dark classic Mickey hides just above the trunk in the branches of the leftmost tree.

Hint 26: You can spot two classic Mickeys on the left side of a fabric mural on the far right side of the rear wall behind the main registration counters. One is below the second maroon line from the top and the other is above the fifth maroon line from the top.

Hint 27: On the registration counter to the far left (as you face the main registration counters), classic Mickeys are in the trees on each side of the front of the counter. Look in the lower tree branches.

Hint 28: A classic Mickey depression is on the face of the grandfather clock in the main lobby.

Hint 29: A classic Mickey hole is in the middle front of a desk, high up under the projecting lip of the desktop. The desk is usually at the rear left of the main lobby.

Hint 30: Telephones near the lobby elevators sport two classic Mickeys each, one above a touchtone button at the lower part of the phone information panel and another at the top of the panel in the tree logo for the Grand Californian hotel. You'll also find the tree-logo classic Mickey on the dials of rotary phones near the lobby.

Hint 31: On a map of the Grand Californian on a wall along a walkway at the left (as you enter) of the main lobby, the Children's Pool area is shaped like a classic Mickey.

Hint 32: In the nearby hallway, classic Mickeys are in the corners of the frame of a painting that hangs on the wall near the restrooms. The painting shows a rocky and mountainous coastline.

Hint: 33 A classic Mickey made of round stones and tilted to the right is in the lower front part of the rock wall on the left side of the lobby fireplace.

Hint 34: A small model of a Disney Cruise Lines' ship is at the right side of the main lobby (as you enter from the front) and near the registration counters. (Note: This model ship may be moved around the lobby from time to time). Classic Mickeys are on the bow and the two smokestacks. A fourth Hidden Mickey is aft: his face is painted on the bottom of the pool toward the stern (rear) end of the ship.

- *Hearthstone Lounge*

Hint 35: Classic Mickey holes repeat near the outer rim of some of the large light fixtures hanging from the ceiling in the Hearthstone Lounge.

- *Walkway to Downtown Disney*

Hint 36: As you start along the walkway to Downtown Disney, turn around and look up to spot a classic Mickey on the Grand Californian logo tree in an upper-story window.

Hint 37: Classic Mickeys adorn each of the Grand Californian tree logos that are embossed on the planters lining the walkway to Downtown Disney.

- *Walkway to Disney California Adventure*

Hint 38: The side panels of the lamps along the walkway to the Disney California Adventure Park entrance are embellished with tree designs. The tallest tree on each panel has a classic Mickey in its lower branches.

- *Disneyland Drive*

Hint 39: The large Grand Californian entrance signs facing Disneyland Drive include the hotel's tree logo with its classic Mickey.

Disney's Paradise Pier Hotel

- *Outside the front entrance*

Hint 40: Classic Mickey impressions are in the gray recessed wall just to the left of the front entrance (as you face the hotel.)

- *Inside the hotel*

Hint 41: A classic Mickey is on the back of a shirt at the lower right of a picture that's hanging on the lobby wall. It's across from the main lobby entrance doors, near the elevators.

Hint 42: Rocks form a (slightly distorted) classic Mickey at the upper right of a painting on the stairwell wall between the first and second floors near the main elevators.

Hint 43: On the second floor, you'll find classic-Mickey wooden cutouts in the trim above the entrances to both Mickey's Beach Workout Room and the Beachcomber Club. (An entrance door to the fitness center also features a large decorative classic-Mickey window.)

Hint 44: At the edges of the blue carpet in the hallways, large clams near starfish form

classic Mickeys with smaller circles for "ears." (Note: Carpets change from time to time, but you can usually find Hidden Mickeys in any new carpets in the hotels.)

Hint 45: On the third floor, classic Mickeys grace the top railings around the swimming pool.

Hint 46: Large partial classic Mickeys top the palm trees along the wall of the Game Room near the lobby elevators.

Hint 47: On a wall across from the Pacific Ballroom, a red classic Mickey reflection is in a photo of a sunset over the water. You see the sun through pier supports.

- Disney's PCH Grill

Hint 48: A multicolored classic Mickey in swirls is woven into the restaurant's carpet.

Hint 49: Small black classic Mickeys hide on diagonal wires on the wall, while a large, black partial classic Mickey hides higher up on the wall near the kitchen.

Hint 50: Black classic Mickeys are on the food lamps hanging in the kitchen area.

Hint 51: A large classic Mickey with the earth as Mickey's head hides in a picture on the wall.

Hint 52: Large black classic Mickeys are near the ceiling in the rear room, one on a red kite and the other on a yellow kite.

Hint 53: Three different surfboards decorating the restaurant's walls shelter classic Mickeys, one in fireworks, one in flowers, and one in black circles at the bottom of the surfboard.

Hint 54: Black partial classic Mickeys hide in the glass panels of each of the double doors at the restaurant entrance.

- *Outside the rear entrance*

Hint 55: Classic Mickeys are atop short poles just outside the rear entrance to the hotel.

Disneyland Hotel

- *Lobby and entrance areas*

Hint 56: In the lobby and registration area, two green classic Mickeys (of different sizes) and a gold classic Mickey are repeated in the carpet.

Hint 57: Full-face Mickeys (frontal view) are repeated in the light gold wallpaper in the central lobby.

Hint 58: Classic Mickeys top the light poles in the main entrance parking lot.

Hint 59: Classic Mickeys are hiding in the middle of the side railings of the luggage carts.

Hint 60: Below the central lobby, look for the room where "Lost and Found" is located. A complete classic Mickey is formed by the silver push panels on a set of swinging doors, while a partial Mickey is on the push panel of the single door marked, "Cast Members Only."

- *Gift shops*

Hint 61: Near the main lobby, side-profile Mickeys are in the blue carpet inside Disney's Fantasia Gift Shop and also inside Donald's Gifts and Sundries.

Hint 62: Small Mickey, Minnie, Donald, and Goofy figures are pasted on the outer glass panels of Donald's Gifts and Sundries shop.

Hint 63: Telephones in nearby hallways each have a classic Mickey above a touchtone button along the lower part of the phone information panel.

- *Guest Services office*

Hint 64: Inside the Guest Services office, you'll find classic Mickeys in four places: in the backs of chairs, on desks (below the desktops), and in two places on the Disney Cruise Line ship model, the smokestacks and the bow. You'll spot the fifth image, Mickey's full face, behind the model's aft (rear) smokestack.

- *Around the hotel complex*

Hint 65: Classic Mickeys are atop dividers between phones in the phone bank area behind a wall with photos near the Convention Center.

Hint 66: Inside the hotel, in the Convention Center area to the right, small classic Mickeys are repeated in the light blue sides of the carpet, while giant gold classic Mickeys adorn its center.

Hint 67: Classic Mickeys of various sizes and colors hide in the carpet in Goofy's Theater, across from Steakhouse 55.

Hint 68: On the floor to the right of Goofy's Kitchen and Steakhouse 55, a tiny gold classic Hidden Mickey hides in the trail of Tinker Bell's pixie dust at the lower right of a blue mosaic of a castle. (For added fun, look up at the umbrellas hanging from the ceiling for decorative Mickey images).

Hint 69: Gold classic Mickeys are atop the ends of the middle handrail on the stairs near Goofy's Kitchen.

Hint 70: On the ceiling at the top of a staircase near Goofy's Kitchen, a large classic Mickey on a blue background is secured by small classic Mickey bolts.

Hint 71: Find the woman wearing a red dress in the right lower section of a stylized painting of Toontown. The two children with her are wearing Mickey ears.

Hint 72: Look at the lower right section of the painting of a scene in front of *Splash Mountain*. From left to right, you can spot three classic Mickeys: a red Mickey balloon, a small white and black Mickey balloon, and a child with Mickey ears at the far right of the painting.

- Near Sleeping Beauty Pavilion

Hint 73: Classic Mickeys are in the red carpet in the hallways near the Sleeping Beauty Pavilion and the Magic Kingdom Ballroom.

Hint 74: On the bank of telephones near the hallway adjacent to the Sleeping Beauty Pavilion, classic Mickeys are on the light covers and Mickey silhouettes are on the dividers between the phones.

Hint 75: Across from the Sleeping Beauty Pavilion, a classic Mickey hides in a painting of a jungle temple. It's on the top front of the hood of a jeep at the lower middle of the painting.

Hint 76: You'll find Mickey's face in the wallpaper and classic Mickeys in the carpets of the hotel's other towers.

Other Mickey Appearances

These Hidden Mickeys won't earn you any points, but you're bound to enjoy them if you're in the right place at the right time to see them.

Look for holiday Hidden Mickeys if you're at Disneyland during the Christmas season, or for that matter, any major holiday.

Other "Hidden" Mickeys – décor and deliberate – appear with some regularity throughout the Disneyland® Resort. Notice the Mickster on Disneyland brochures, maps and flags, Cast Member name tags, guest room keys, pay telephones and phone books, and restaurant and store receipts. The restaurants sometimes offer classic Mickey butter and margarine pats, pancakes and waffles, and pizzas and pasta, as well as Mickey napkins. They also arrange dishes and condiments to form classic Mickeys. Some condiment containers are even shaped like Mickey. Road signs on Disneyland property may sport Mickey ears, and Disneyland vehicles and monorails may display Mickey Mouse insignia.

Cleaning personnel will often spray the ground, windows, furniture, and other items with three circles of cleaning solution (a classic Mickey) before the final cleansing. Or they may leave three wet Mickey Mouse circles or other Disney character images on the pavement after mopping! Mickey even decorates manhole covers, survey markers, and utility covers in the ground, as you've probably already discovered for yourself.

Enjoy all these Mickeys as you enjoy Disneyland. And if you want to take some home with you, rest assured that you can always find "Hidden" Mickeys on souvenir mugs, merchandise bags and boxes, T-shirts, and Christmas tree ornaments sold in the Disneyland shops. So even when you're far away from Disneyland, you can continue to enjoy Hidden Mickeys.

To enjoy a Hidden Mickey from above, check out Google Earth and find the classic Mickey created by two sidewalks on either side of Disneyland Drive approaching Katella Avenue—below and just to the right of Disney's Paradise Pier Hotel in the Google Earth image.

To access the image, go to GoogleEarth (download the program from GoogleEarth.com) and "Fly to" Disneyland, California by clicking on the magnifying glass next to the destination. Then scroll with your mouse to the left and down until you're just below the Paradise Pier hotel, and you'll see the palm-outlined Hidden Mickey. (The palm-lined sidewalks form the head and ears).

It's a distorted image, but the voters on my website liked it as a Hidden Mickey. I think you will, too.

CHAPTER 6

My Favorite Hidden Mickeys

In this field guide, I've described nearly 400 Hidden Mickeys at the Disneyland Resort. I enjoy every one of them, but the following are extra special to me. They're special because of their uniqueness, their deep camouflage (which makes them especially hard to find), or the "Eureka!" response they elicit when I spot them—or any combination of the above. Here then are my Favorite Hidden Mickeys at Disneyland. I apologize to you if your favorite Hidden Mickey is not (yet) on the list below.

My Top Ten

1. Conductor Mickey. Check the registration counter at Disney's Grand Californian Hotel & Spa and marvel at this magnificent (but tiny) rendition of Mickey conducting an imagined musical symphony for the dancing bears nearby. You'll feel like singing along! (Clue 22, Chap. 4)

2. Randall's Mickey. In the *Monster's Inc.* ride, Hollywood Pictures Backlot, Disney California Adventure Park, the little girl Boo pounds monster Randall with a bat. As Randall (who looks like a lizard and changes color like a chameleon) changes colors, a classic Mickey sometimes appears on his belly. This great Mickey image is intermittent, so stare long and hard at poor Randall, and don't wince! (Clue 28, Chap. 3)

3. Mr. Toad's Door Mickey, Fantasyland, Disneyland. You mustn't miss this marvelous Mickey image on the right door (lower left corner) of the third set of doors you crash through at the beginning of *Mr. Toad's Wild Ride*. Try not to wreck your car looking for it! (Clue 89, Chap. 2)

4. Golf Ball Mickey. At *Soarin' Over California*, Golden State, California Adventure, keep your eyes peeled for this rotating

classic Mickey on a golf ball. He's visible for only a second. Don't blink! (Clue 15, Chap. 3)

5. Mickey Smiling Out From A Tree. Out front of Disney's Grand Californian Hotel & Spa, observe a three-quarter view of Mickey's face peering out from between the branches of a tree on a ceramic panel on one of the columns. Yes, he's smiling at you! (Clue 19, Chap. 4)

6. Winnie the Pooh's Tree Mickey. As you take off in your beehive in *The Many Adventures of Winnie the Pooh*, Critter Country, Disneyland Park, squint to your right to admire this subtle classic Mickey in the bark of a tree. When you see it, you'll want to bounce like Tigger! (Clue 23, Chap. 2)

7. Big Ben Mickey. A side view of Mickey's face is below you in a window of Big Ben during *Peter Pan's Flight* in Disneyland's Fantasyland. Look back to spot Mickey in London! (Clue 10, Chap. 2)

8. Mark Twain Mickey. Make a special trip to Frontierland, Disneyland, to find Mickey on a steamboat. He's standing by two well-dressed women on the lower deck. Mickey in a tux! (Clue 47, Chap. 2)

9. Jungle Mickey. Study this wall painting in the Disneyland Hotel, across from the Sleeping Beauty Pavilion. Mickey is on the top front of the hood of a jeep. This is one adventurous Mickey! (Clue 75, Chap. 4)

10. Sunset Mickey. Journey to Disney's Paradise Pier Hotel to gawk at the sunset classic Mickey in the photo on the wall near the Pacific Ballroom. How did they do that? (Clue 47, Chap. 4)

Ten Honorable Mentions

1. Nemo Rock Mickey. Make a special effort to chase down this classic Mickey in a rock wall near the elevator for the Disneyland Monorail in Tomorrowland, near *Finding Nemo Submarine Voyage*. You won't regret it! (Clue 106, Chap. 2)

2. Pinocchio Ship Mickey. Pinocchio is a classic, and so is this hard-to-spot, elegant classic Mickey on a model ship's case in *Pinocchio's Daring Journey*, Fantasyland, Disneyland. Ahoy, Mickey! (Clue 95, Chap. 2)

3. Clock Mickey. A subtle classic Mickey impression adorns the face of the grandfather clock in the lobby of Disney's Grand Californian Hotel & Spa. You'll be impressed! (Clue 28, Chap. 4)

4. Tiny Sign Mickey. *Splash Mountain*, Critter Country, Disneyland, is even more awesome if you stop to peer at the tiny classic Mickey in the wood of the warning sign that you'll find in the first part of the outside entrance queue. Wow! (Clue 51, Chap. 2)

5. Skyline Mickey. At the beginning of your ride on *Monsters, Inc. Mike & Sulley to the Rescue!*, Hollywood Backlot Pictures, Disney California Adventure, admire Mickey in the skyline to your left. A skyline will never be the same! (Clue 26, Chap. 3)

6. Spotlight Mickey. Inside *The Twilight Zone Tower of Terror* in California Adventure's Hollywood Backlot Pictures, veer to the left lower elevator loading area to stand under this Mickey in lights. Look up and be amazed! (Clue 20, Chap. 3)

7. Lava Mickey. Along the *Toy Story Midway Mania!* ride, Paradise Pier, California Adventure, don't overlook Mickey in the lava behind a middle-level balloon. You have to pop the balloon to see Mickey. (Clue 3, Chap. 3)

8. Pixie Dust Mickey. At the Disneyland Hotel, near Goofy's Kitchen, show your friends the tiny classic Mickey in Tinker Bell's pixie dust in the castle floor mosaic. You and your friends may feel like floating! (Clue 68, Chap. 4)

9. Luggage Hidden Images. Along the entrance queue for *Star Tours—The Adventures Continue*, Tomorrowland, Disneyland, linger with the robot scanning luggage to spot Mickey and other characters. It's an X-ray Mickey! (Clue 110, Chap. 2)

10. Dalmatian Mickey. In Mickey's Toontown, Disneyland, push the doorbell for the Fire Department and stand back to greet the Dalmatian and his Hidden Mickey above you. This puppy needs a treat! (Clue 86, Chap. 2)

Don't Stop Now!

Hidden Mickey mania is contagious. The benign pastime of searching out Hidden Mickeys has escalated into a bona fide vacation mission for many Disneyland fans. I'm happy to add my name to the list of hunters. Searching for images of the Main Mouse can enhance a solo trip to the parks or a vacation for the entire family. Little ones delight in spotting and greeting Mickey Mouse characters in the parks and restaurants. As children grow, the Hidden Mickey game is a natural evolution of their fondness for the Mouse.

Join the search! With alert eyes and mind, you can spot Hidden Mickey classics and new ones waiting to be found. Even beginners have happened upon a new, unreported Hidden Mickey or two. As new attractions open and older ones get refurbished, new Hidden Mickeys await discovery.

The Disney entertainment phenomenon is unique in many ways, and Hidden Mickey mania is one manifestation of Disney's universal appeal. Join in the fun! Maybe I'll see you at Disneyland, marveling (like me) at the Hidden Gems. They're waiting patiently for you to discover them.

Notes

Index to Mickey's Hiding Places

Note: This Index includes only those rides, restaurants, shops, hotels and other places in the Disneyland Resort that harbor confirmed Hidden Mickeys. So if the attraction you're looking for isn't included, Mickey isn't hiding there. Or if he is, I haven't yet spotted him.

— *Steve Barrett*

The following abbreviations appear in this Index:

DL – Disneyland Park
CA – Disney California Adventure Park
DD – Downtown Disney District
RH – Resort Hotel

A

"a bug's land" (CA) 72
    Heimlich's Chew Chew Train 72
Adventureland (DL) 30, 33–34
    Enchanted Tiki Room 34
    Indiana Jones Adventure 30
    Jungle Cruise 33
    Tarzan's Treehouse 33–34
Alice in Wonderland (DL) 36
Animation Academy (CA) 75
Animation Building (CA). *See* Disney Animation Building (CA)
Ariel's Grotto (CA) 74
    across from 74
Ariel's Undersea Adventure (CA). *See* The Little Mermaid (CA)
ASIMO robot show area (DL) 39–40
Astro Orbitor (DL) 40
Autopia (DL) 33

B

Baker's Field Bakery (CA) 77
Bakery Tour, The (CA) 74
Big Thunder Mountain Railroad (DL) 29
Big Thunder Ranch (DL) 32–33
Blue Ribbon Bakery (DL) 42
Blue Sky Cellar, Walt Disney Imagineering (CA) 74
    across from 74
Briar Patch (DL) 32
bug's land (CA). *See* "a bug's land"
Buzz Lightyear Astro Blasters (DL) 28–29

C

California Screamin' (CA) 67
"Captain EO" (DL) 40
Casey Jr. Circus Train (DL) 37
Castle Heraldry Shoppe (DL) 38
Clarabelle's Frozen Yogurt (DL) 36
Critter Country (DL) 29–30, 32
    Briar Patch store 32
    Splash Mountain 32
    The Many Adventures of Winnie the Pooh 29–30

D

D Street (DD) 91
Disney Animation Building (CA) 75–76
    Animation Academy 75
    Off the Page 76
    Sorcerer's Workshop 75–76
Disney Junior—Live on Stage! (CA) 72–73
Disney Vault 28 (DD) 91
Disney's Grand Californian Hotel & Spa. *See* Grand
    Californian Hotel & Spa, Disney's
Disney's Paradise Pier Hotel. *See* Paradise Pier Hotel,
    Disney's
Disney's PCH Grill (RH) 98
Disneyland Hotel 99–101
    Guest Services office 100
    lobby and entrance areas 99
    main lobby gift shops 99

Disneyland Hotel, cont'd.
near Goofy's Kitchen 100
near Sleeping Beauty Pavilion 101
outside the front entrance 99
Disneyland Monorail elevator in Tomorrowland (DL)
near 38
Disneyland Railroad (DL)
Main Street Station 42–43
Downtown Disney District 91, 94
D Street 91
Disney Vault 28 91
Marceline's Confectionery 91
Naples Ristorante e Pizzeria 91, 94
Quiksilver 94
Studio Disney 365 91
World of Disney 94
Dream Home (DL) 39

E

Emporium (DL) 42
Enchanted Tiki Room (DL) 34
Engine-Ears Toys (CA) 77
Entrance areas
Disneyland Hotel 99
Disneyland Park 25, 43
Downtown Disney District 94
entrance plaza between the parks 77–78
Frontierland entrance walkway (DL) 40
Grand Californian Hotel & Spa, Disney's 95, 97
Mickey's Toontown (DL) 34
Paradise Pier Hotel, Disney's 97, 98–99
security bag check area (DL) 25
Entrance plaza between the theme parks 77–78

F

Fantasmic! (DL) 43
Fantasyland (DL) 25, 28, 36–38
Alice in Wonderland 36
Casey Jr. Circus Train 37
Castle Heraldry Shoppe 38
"it's a small world" 37

Fantasyland (DL), cont'd.
King Arthur Carrousel 38
Mad Hatter 38
Matterhorn Bobsleds 25, 28
Mr. Toad's Wild Ride 36
Peter Pan's Flight 28
Pinocchio's Daring Journey 37
Pixie Hollow Meet and Greet 28
Snow White's Scary Adventures 36–37
Storybook Land Canal Boats 37
Finding Nemo Submarine Voyage (DL)
Marine Observation Outpost 38
Monorail exit, near 38
Fireworks show (DL) 43
Frontierland (DL) 29, 31–33, 40–41
Big Thunder Mountain Railroad 29
Big Thunder Ranch 32–33
Frontierland Shootin' Exposition 41
Mark Twain Riverboat 31–32
Pioneer Mercantile 41
Raft to Tom Sawyer Island 32
Rancho del Zocalo Restaurante 41
River Belle Terrace 41
Sailing Ship Columbia 31–32
The Golden Horseshoe 31
Tom Sawyer Island 32
walkway to 40
Frontierland Shootin' Exposition (DL) 41

G

Gadget's Go Coaster (DL) 34
Gibson Girl Ice Cream Parlor (DL) 42
Golden Horseshoe, The (DL) 31
Golden State (CA) 70, 74–75
Grizzly River Run area 75
Redwood Creek Challenge Trail 74–75
Rushin' River Outfitters 75
Soarin' Over California 70
Taste Pilots' Grill 75
The Bakery Tour 74
Tow Mater's Greeting Area 74
Walt Disney Imagineering Blue Sky Cellar 74

Goofy's Kitchen, near (RH) 100
Grand Californian Hotel & Spa, Disney's 95–97
  Hearthstone Lounge 96
  lobby area 95–96
  outside the main entrance 95
Greetings from California (CA) 76–77
Grizzly River Run (CA)
  fence near entrance to 75

H

Haunted Mansion (DL) 31
Hearthstone Lounge (RH) 96
Heimlich's Chew Chew Train (CA) 72
Hollywood Pictures Backlot (CA) 70–73, 75–76
  Animation Academy 75
  Disney Animation Building 75–76
  Disney Junior—Live on Stage! 72–73
  Hyperion Theater 72
  Monsters, Inc. 71–72
  MuppetVision 3D 72
  Schmoozies 76
  Studio Store 76
  The Twilight Zone Tower of Terror 70–71
Hyperion Theater (CA) 72

I

Innoventions (DL) 39–40
  ASIMO robot show area 39–40
  Dream Home area 39
  outside wall murals 40
Indiana Jones Adventure (DL) 30
"it's a small world" (DL) 37

J

Jumpin' Jellyfish (CA) 73
Jungle Cruise (DL) 33

K

King Arthur Carrousel (DL) 38

L

Little Mermaid, The (CA) 70

M

Mad Hatter shop (DL) 38
Main Street Magic Shop (DL) 42
Main Street, U.S.A. (DL) 41–43
  Blue Ribbon Bakery 42
  Disneyland Railroad Station 42–43
  Emporium 42
  fruit cart 41
  Gibson Girl Ice Cream Parlor 42
  Main Street Cinema 42
  Main Street Magic Shop 42
  Market House 41–42
  Penny Arcade 42
  Photo Supply Company 41
  Plaza Inn 41
  Silhouette Studio 41
Main Street Cinema (DL) 42
Man Hat n' Beach (CA) 73
Many Adventures of Winnie the Pooh, The (DL) 29–30
Marceline's Confectionery (DD) 91
Marine Observation Outpost (DL) 38
Market House (DL) 41–42
Mark Twain Riverboat (DL) 31–32
Matterhorn Bobsleds (DL) 25, 28
Mickey & Friends Parking Structure 94
  tram path to/from 95
Mickey's House (DL) 34–35
  outside 35
Mickey's Movie Barn (DL) 35
Mickey's Toontown (DL) 34–36
  Clarabelle's Frozen Yogurt 36
  entrance area 34
  Fire Department 36
  Gadget's Go Coaster 34
  Mickey's House 34–35
  Mickey's Movie Barn 35
  Minnie's House 35–36
  Post Office 36

Minnie's House (DL) 35–36
outside 35
telephone hut near 36
Monsters, Inc. (CA) 71–72
Mr. Toad's Wild Ride (DL) 36
MuppetVision 3D (CA) 72

N

Naples Ristorante e Pizzeria (DD) 91, 94
New Orleans Square (DL) 30–31
Haunted Mansion 31
Pirates of the Caribbean 30–31

O

Off the Page (CA) 76

P

Parade, afternoon (DL) 33
Paradise Bay (CA)
World of Color 78
Paradise Pier (CA) 67, 70, 73–74
Ariel's Grotto 74
California Screamin' 67
Jumpin' Jellyfish 73
Man Hat n' Beach 73
Point Mugu Tattoo 73
promenade 73
Sideshow Shirts 73
The Little Mermaid 70
Toy Story Midway Mania! 67
Treasures in Paradise 74
Paradise Pier Hotel, Disney's 97–99
Disney's PCH Grill 98
outside the front entrance 97
outside the rear entrance 98–99
PCH Grill, Disney's (RH) 98
Penny Arcade (DL) 42
Peter Pan's Flight (DL) 28
Photo Supply Company (DL) 41
Pinocchio's Daring Journey (DL) 37

Pioneer Mercantile (DL) 41
Pirates of the Caribbean (DL) 30–31
Pixie Hollow Meet and Greet (DL) 28
Plaza Inn (DL) 41
Point Mugu Tattoo (CA) 73

Q

Quiksilver (DD) 94

R

Raft to Tom Sawyer Island (DL) 32
Rancho del Zocalo Restaurante (DL) 41
Redd Rockett's Pizza Port (DL) 40
Redwood Creek Challenge Trail (CA) 74–75
River Belle Terrace (DL) 41
Rushin' River Outfitters (CA) 75

S

Sailing Ship Columbia (DL) 31–32
Schmoozies (CA) 76
Sideshow Shirts (CA) 73
Silhouette Studio (DL) 41
Snow White's Scary Adventures (DL) 36–37
Soarin' Over California (CA) 70
Sorcerer's Workshop (CA) 75–76
Space Mountain (DL) 29
Splash Mountain (DL) 32
Star Tours—The Adventures Continue (DL) 38–39
Star Trader, The (DL) 40
Storybook Land Canal Boats (DL) 37
Studio Disney 365 (DD) 91
Studio Store (CA) 76
Sun Fountain (CA) 76
Sunshine Plaza (CA) 76–77
    Baker's Field Bakery 77
    Engine-Ears Toys 77
    Greetings from California 76–77
    Sun Fountain 76

T

Tarzan's Treehouse (DL) 33–34
Taste Pilots' Grill (CA) 75
The Bakery Tour (CA) 74
The Golden Horseshoe (DL) 31
The Little Mermaid—Ariel's Undersea Adventure (CA) 70
The Many Adventures of Winnie the Pooh (DL) 29–30
The Star Trader (DL) 40
The Twilight Zone Tower of Terror (CA) 70–71
Tomorrowland (DL) 28–29, 33, 38–40
- Astro Orbitor 40
- Autopia 33
- Buzz Lightyear Astro Blasters 28–29
- "Captain EO" 40
- elevator for the Disneyland Monorail, near 38
- Finding Nemo Submarine Voyage (DL) 38
  - Marine Observation Outpost 38
  - Monorail elevator near 38
- Innoventions 39–40
- Redd Rockett's Pizza Port 40
- Space Mountain 29
- Star Tours—The Adventures Continue 38–39
- The Star Trader 40

Tom Sawyer Island (DL) 32
Toontown Fire Department (DL) 36
Toontown Post Office (DL) 36
Tower of Terror, The Twilight Zone (CA) 70–71
Tow Mater's Greeting Area (CA) 74
Toy Story Midway Mania! (CA) 67
Treasures in Paradise (CA) 74
Twilight Zone Tower of Terror, The (CA) 70–71

W

Walt Disney Imagineering Blue Sky Cellar (CA) 74
Winnie the Pooh, The Many Adventures of (DL) 29–30
World of Color (CA) 78
World of Disney (DD) 94

www.intrepidtraveler.com